ALONG CAME TSAKANI

KAGISO MODUPE

First published by Kwarts Publishers, 2018

Copyright © 2018 by Kagiso Modupe
www.kagisomodupe.co.za

ISBN 978-0-620-78817-5
E-book ISBN 978-0-620-78818-2

Editor: Phillipa Mitchell

Additional copies of this book can be purchased from
Red Pepper Online at www.redpepperonline.co.za,
and from Amazon.com and all good online bookstores
worldwide.

To all the women who ever wondered what happened

CHAPTER 1

Muzi woke up with a start, his chest heaving. While he waited for the thudding to die down, he laughed quietly to himself. What had startled him awake was not the sound of an intruder, moving and breathing as it made its way through the house. No. What had startled him awake was his two-year-old daughter, Lethu, crying at the top of her lungs in the bedroom next door.

He reached out across the mahogany bed stand, fumbling for his mobile phone, almost toppling the silver wafer-wrapped lamp off the smooth glass surface. It was twenty minutes past two. Past midnight. Pre-dawn.

Muzi had been working late into the night and he had barely been asleep for a full three hours. He had converted the third bedroom into a makeshift office-cum-reading room shortly after they had moved in, dividing it with a beautiful handmade plywood screen that he had painted a glossy black.

His eyes were itchy, craving sleep. He was a lighter sleeper than his wife Tshidi was, and he would usually be the first to hear his daughter when she woke up in the odd hours of the night, screaming for attention. She was in that temperamental stage of growth known as the *terrible twos*, and middle-of-the-night tantrums were just one of many ways in which she would torment her adoring parents.

Lethu was already showing signs of being *daddy's girl*, often refusing to be rocked back to sleep by her mother, stubbornly asking for her father by name. "*Mubi!*" she would cry out, unable to pronounce Muzi. *Mubi*, literally translated, meant ugly, and Tshidi would go to great lengths to tease her husband about his nickname. She knew that he would not take offence, because he was, without a doubt, a handsome man.

"This must be the first time in your whole life that somebody has called you ugly," Tshidi would joke, "She's fixing you up for me nicely. Men who know they are good looking can be a problem!"

Muzi would laugh and play along. "*Hawu*, so handsome men can be a problem?" he would ask, laughing, "Exactly how do you know this? Didn't you say that I was your first handsome prince after kissing a few frogs?"

And they would both collapse in fits of laughter

Muzi looked over at his wife. She was in a deep sleep; peaceful, beautiful, and breathing with a quiet, gentle rhythm. He would have to see to the baby himself.

Cradling his daughter in his arms and humming sweet nothings in her ear, he felt blessed, and for that, he was grateful. He looked around at the room that he and Tshidi had converted into a nursery. The walls and the ceilings were painted in bright, vivid colours. He reminded himself again, smiling, that he was blessed with a happy little family, and he thanked God for it.

It did not take long before Muzi could tell that little Lethu was fast asleep, and he gently lowered his daughter back into her cherry-coloured bed, sculpted with little wooden bars all around it. He walked silently, barefoot, back to the master bedroom, the cold tiles pressing against the soles of his feet. Slipping back under the covers, Muzi was restless, and he began to wonder how long it would be before he would fall asleep again.

Lying on his back, Tshidi turned around in her sleep, away from him, her forearm grazing against his erection, sending hot arrows of desire piercing through his loins. Muzi moved closer towards her, his hard manhood pressing against the soft, warm groove of her buttocks. He kissed her gently down her long, slim neck. He had always said that it was the most graceful neck that he had ever laid his eyes on.

Tshidi moved in her sleep and Muzi reached around her waist, his hand fumbling hand upwards beneath one of her breasts. He circled her nipple with his fingers and felt it grow hard. Aching for her, he pulled her closer towards him, ready to turn her around.

"Baby, stop," she murmured drowsily, taking his hand from her breast and turning over onto her back, "I'll be sleepy in the morning and at work, baby. Please stop." She kissed him on the cheek and shifted her body further away from him, while Muzi considered persisting. She looked so peaceful and tranquil, he thought, the slant of her left eye above her prominent cheekbone, both translucent in the glow of moonlight which peeked in through a gap in the crimson curtains, spilling onto her face. Muzi retracted his lean, muscular arms, sighed deeply, and gave up on his quest.

Returning from the bathroom several minutes later, he chuckled to himself in the passage, realising that he was spending considerably more time engaging in *the armed struggle*, as he and his friends referred to it during their varsity days. Here he was, married, but still caught up in the same struggle. Such was life, he thought, a little sourly, but he knew that - today of all days - he would have to maintain a cheerful mood. He had a business proposition – unrelated to his job - to present during his lunch hour. He would not be doing himself any favours if he allowed himself to feel demotivated by moping through the morning. No, he would need to keep a positive mindset well past noon if he was going to make a success of his lunch hour meeting. His family's future depended on it.

Being an entrepreneur had been his goal for most of his adult life, and even more so now that he had a family to provide for. It was one thing to be employed, but Muzi's ultimate goal was to be an employer; to empower others and to change the face of corporate ownership in a country where it was said that Black people were now *free*.

Muzi thanked God for his middle management job at an advertising agency in Ekurhuleni, especially considering the employment situation being in steady decline in the now *free* South Africa. He planned to become his own boss before he turned forty. He always remembered the words of his late uncle *Bab'ncane* Theophilus, his father's younger brother, and a schoolteacher, who had taken Muzi in and raised him after his father had died during his final year of primary school.

"Son," he would say, "Nobody ever became rich from being employed. An employee works to make his employers rich, not himself." Those words had left a lasting impression on Muzi. He needed to, wanted to, and *had to* rise to the occasion. As an entrepreneur at heart, he was always turning ideas over in his head.

Muzi was thirty-five, and every day that he found himself working under somebody else's employ left him feeling as if he was running out of time; that with each passing day he was placing the welfare of his family in jeopardy. Although they were a two-income family, the truth of the matter was that they were really just getting by, unable to save or invest in any meaningful way, just like many of the other middle-aged middle-class Black couples in their neighbourhood.

Since getting married, Muzi had cut down on most of his pastimes and habits that involved spending money, especially after Lethu was born. When Lethu was only eight months old, Muzi and Tshidi agreed that Tshidi should go back to work and that they would hire a nanny to look after the baby. Their verbal agreement was that Tshidi would be responsible for paying the nanny, but, more often than not, Muzi found himself having to foot this bill as well; Tshidi usually had one or other 'emergency' that she needed to provide for in her extended family.

Muzi had taught himself, quickly and out of necessity, to draw the line when it came to putting the needs of *his* immediate family before those of his extended

family, but he felt that the same could not be said for
Tshidi.

Muzi was fond of his in-laws; he was quite friendly
with his father-in-law, and he had a close relationship
with his mother-in-law and all five of Tshidi's siblings.
Muzi cared for his in-laws as much as he cared for his
own relatives, and he valued the close relationship his
wife had with her family, but Tshidi's family was a
constant strain on his young family's coffers.

There always seemed to be a relative that Tshidi "had
to help", and Muzi, who disliked arguing with his
wife, usually found himself making up for the
shortfalls in the household budget.

What was a man to do? he thought. He could take it up
with the family elders on either side, but they were
part of the problem, and Muzi didn't want to put
further strain on the relationship between his mother
and his wife; a relationship that was a bit tense at the
best of times.

His mother often complained to Muzi, telling him that he was spoiling Tshidi and that he allowed her to get her way too often, but he always came to his wife's defence.

Fortunately, Muzi's mother and her husband lived some distance away – it was a five-hour drive to be exact, and in another province - whereas Tshidi's family were all close by, and had become part of the normal, almost daily routine of Muzi's family life. Tshidi's mother was at the couple's home every other day.

Muzi, despite being the problem solver, could not bring himself to tell Tshidi that she would, at some point, simply have to learn to say no to her relatives. He had raised the issue with her several times, but always let it go.

Of course, they were not the only couple dealing with the burden of an extended family, together with the real needs and sometimes-unrealistic expectations that came with it. *Black Tax*, for the emerging Black middle class, was a very real thing, and completely unavoidable. It was one of the remnants of Apartheid; a system designed to suppress the lives and the potential of Black people, creating a nation of privileged white employers serviced by poorly educated black workers.

Black tax was a fact of life. There were always sisters and cousins and uncles and aunts and nephews and nieces who looked to their relatively better-off family members for assistance. Those family members were always there, either somewhere far away in the *rurals*, or close by in the townships.

After his father had passed away and his mother had remarried, Muzi's own extended family was not as close-knit as that of Tshidi's. Living in Johannesburg, Muzi was separated from his paternal family by distance, with most of his relatives living in Kwa-Zulu Natal. He usually saw them only at Christmas time.

Although he loved his mother dearly, and despite the fact that he had been raised by his uncle and his aunt and had only spent holidays with his mother, his primary responsibility was to his wife and daughter. His mother, along with his half-siblings and everybody else in his extended family, knew this. It was something he had always tried to make crystal clear in both his actions and his words. Did the Holy Bible not state that a man would leave the house of his mother and father and cleave to his wife? That in marriage the two would become one?

Muzi was hopeful that everything would ultimately resolve itself, and the solution was obvious to him: he had to make more money. He liked giving, and he liked being able to give. Money would make everybody's life easier, and he was determined to make it. He was a provider and a problem-solver. He was not a complainer. This was the practical solution that he applied to every problem that was material in nature.

Although his workplace was close to their home in Crystal Park, Muzi usually left before Tshidi in the mornings, not because he needed to, but because he had developed a habit of arriving at the office an hour earlier than was necessary. He liked to use the quiet time to map out his endless business ideas, alone in the open plan office.

Tshidi worked at a small law firm in Fordsburg, a town on the outskirts of the city which had not been overrun by the larger retail stores. It was also a place where you could find the best curry in all of Johannesburg. In their early days as a couple, unable to afford a second car, Muzi would drop Tshidi at work and then drive all the way back to the other side of the city to his place of work.

These daily commutes had become somewhat taxing on the young couple, but Muzi had surprised Tshidi on their first wedding anniversary with a snazzy little Ford Figo, decked out in baby pink, with bright yellow and red flame-coloured emojis on the doors. Since that day, mornings in the Zondi household had become a great deal easier.

But today was different; Tshidi was kissing him goodbye and heading into the morning traffic before

Muzi had even finished getting dressed. He had not slept well, and, even after showering, his eyes were still stinging from a lack of sleep.

As he dressed, he found himself going over the proposal that he would be making to his potential investors later that day over lunch. He caught sight of his reflection in the mirror. He looked puffy-faced and red-eyed. This was a bad start to what *had* to be a good day.

CHAPTER 2

Muzi was grateful for his job, but his work environment kept him preoccupied with his future plans. His industry was crying out for change. Guys like Muzi continued to find themselves reporting to white account executives and creative directors at white-owned advertising agencies, despite the fact that both the market and the consumer demographics had changed.

Black guys like Muzi often found their decisions being overruled by white execs who had a limited understanding of the Black consumer. It was clear to Muzi that the ownership of advertising agencies was still caught up in the past, and he was relentless in his pursuit of a stake in a Black-owned agency.

It was more than simply a dream that he would, one day, head up a Black-owned agency; it was his destiny. As a result, he was extremely committed to his work; he wanted to understand everything that was involved in running an advertising business. He performed his work with excellence because he knew that it was preparing him for greater things. When he prayed, he prayed to God for the strength and the opportunity to become an employer, to make a difference and leave a lasting legacy.

Muzi did not see himself as being overly ambitious; he simply believed that he had a duty to ensure that he lifted his brothers and sisters in the Black community up, instead of focusing just on himself.

His lunchtime meeting that day was one of many possibilities that he was pursuing with potential partners and investors. It had gone well and Muzi was pleased with the potential results of their discussions. The investors were involved in the mining industry and seemed keen to invest in his venture. Things were falling into place. His vision was beginning to take shape. He was hopeful about the future and what it held, both professionally, and for his family.

Over and above this positive news, Muzi had – during his lunchtime meeting - managed to set up a job interview for one of Tshidi's younger brothers, Tumelo. One of the investors had been impressed by the young man's CV. Muzi could hardly wait to get home to break to the news to Tshidi. She worried endlessly about her youngest sibling, an engineering graduate who was in his third year of being unemployed for three years, despite a relentless search for work, with countrywide job applications.

After his lunch meeting, Muzi immersed himself in his work in an effort to compensate for his distracted morning. He had an important pitch to make to an important client the following day. He worked an hour later than usual, avoiding peak hour traffic, and planned to add some finishing touches to his pitch at home later that evening. Tshidi had taken the following day off work because she was taking Lethu for a scheduled check-up with the paediatrician at noon, and he knew that she wouldn't mind giving him some space and time in his study.

Because Muzi usually arrived home a little earlier than Tshidi during the week, he didn't mind cooking supper. He would also have his best father-daughter quality time, especially the part that involved bathing Lethu, even if it involved a great deal of floor mopping once she had finished splashing around. He had read somewhere once that there were two types of kids: those who liked being in the water and those who didn't. His daughter was definitely a water baby, and she knew, with a child's unerring intuition, that playing and splashing around in the bath was a great deal more fun – not to mention permissible - when Daddy was doing the bathing.

Driving home that evening, he remembered that Tshidi had worked half day. His thoughts of bathing Lethu and preparing dinner were interrupted by the beeping of his cell phone in its hands-free kit. Tshidi's number flashed on the screen and her beautiful face came into view.

"Hi, honey," said Muzi, in the tender tone of voice he used only with his wife.

"Hello, my handsome, clever kind hunk of a husband!' she replied warmly, "Where are you?"

Muzi smiled and chuckled at the thought of how well he knew her. His lovely wife was in full *can-you-do-me-a-favour-sweetheart* mode.

"Okay, okay, out with it," he teased, "What am I paying for this time, my love?"

They both laughed.

It was nothing; she was in the mood for lasagne and she didn't feel like cooking. He promised to stop by at their favourite Italian eatery and buy dinner.

"I'll be home soon, gimme thirty minutes," he said, pressing down on the accelerator as the traffic light turned green, and then added, "I love you mama ka Lethu." [1]

"You're a star!" giggled Tshidi, "See you soon my love, baba ka Lethu." [2]

What was it that his childhood friend Tebza had said the first time Muzi introduced Tshidi - who was then Muzi's girlfriend - a few years earlier? He had told Muzi that he had "hit the jackpot"; that's how strikingly beautiful Tshidi was.

She was a stunner, a ten-out-of-ten; a sentiment expressed by many of his friends whenever the talk veered towards wives and girlfriends. Muzi was used to hearing the words *"Wabamba iLotto daar, sbali,"* [3] and his heart swelled with pride and joy every time.

Driving into the underground parking of Lakeside Mall to order the lasagne, he found himself saying it

---

[1] Mother of Lethu

[2] Father of Lethu

[3] "You hit the jackpot, brother-in-law"

out loud, *"Ushade nes'madzadza, boy."* You married a stunner, man.

Muzi skipped out of his sleek BMW and made for the stairs, a bounce in his step and a smile on his lips.

Later that evening, after adding the finishing touches to his pitch, Muzi retired to bed. He was tired, and Tshidi was on her phone. She was always on her phone, WhatsApping with her close circle of girlfriends. They were a tight clique, having grown up in the same neighbourhood and attended the same schools, but *yesses man* they were always WhatsApping *jong*!

"You need to give that poor phone a rest," Muzi said, half-jokingly, slipping in under the sheets beside her. The TV in the bedroom was on - one of Tshidi's beloved Housewives of some place or another - but she was not really watching; she was busy texting.

"LOL," said Tshidi, and continued to text.

"You see?" Muzi retorted, teasingly, "You're even talking like you're texting."

Tshidi laughed and then put the phone away after a few minutes. He cupped her face in his hands as she turned towards him.

"I miss you," he said. The question was playful.

She giggled and tickled him in the ribs. "How can you miss me when I'm here?"

Even though Muzi was exhausted and Tshidi seemed to be just going through the motions, they made love. It was tired, mechanical, dutiful sex that left a silence hanging in the air afterwards. He fell asleep while noticing, drowsily, that Tshidi was reaching for her phone; that ever-present Whatsapp again.

"Baby, tsoga! Tsoga, baby. Muzi, vuka!" [4]Muzi awoke with a start. Tshidi was sitting up in bed, looking as worried as hell. She handed him her phone and asked him to read the text message. It was from Tshidi's

---

[4] "Baby, wake up! Wake up baby. Muzi, wake up!"

mother, stating simply that Tshidi's youngest brother had been arrested.

"Mama called first, and then I asked her to send an SMS, baby," Tshidi said, sniffing and tearing up. Muzi took her into his arms, kissing her forehead and wiping away her tears. He was in full problem-solving mode now. He quickly dialled his mother-in-law from his phone.

"Mama, bambambele kuphi umfana?" Where are they holding him?

If Tumelo had been arrested, the first thing to do would be to find out at which police station he was being held. The second would be to drive there and find out what the hell was going on.

The only information his mother-in-law could give him was that Tumelo had called to say he had been arrested somewhere in Jozi, but the call had been abruptly terminated. His phone had been off ever since.

"Perhaps his battery died," thought Muzi.

He quickly got dressed. It was half-past one in the morning. He explained to a teary-eyed and distraught Tshidi that he would have to go and fetch her father in Daveyton – Tumelo still lived at home - and that together they would then have to establish where Tumelo was being held, and then proceed to sort out this whole mess. Muzi knew that his wife was panicking. This very same younger bro was meant to attend an interview later that morning, the interview that Muzi had organised for him.

"It's gonna be fine my sweetness," Muzi reassured her, "We'll find him. Don't stress." He gave her a tight, comforting hug, and then planted a kiss on her mouth, her cheek, and her forehead, before he left the house.

Muzi's *babezala* (father in law) explained that Tumelo had left at around six o'clock the previous evening. "I gave him my car keys, son," he explained, "He was going to meet some friends in Jozi, at Maboneng, and he promised to be back by ten. We started getting worried when midnight came with no word from him. It's so unlike him," the old man rationalised, "You know that Tumelo is a well-behaved boy. I mean, it's the only reason that I don't mind letting him use my car."

Muzi listened and tried to map out the scenario that might have played out. Tumelo could have been arrested anywhere between Jozi and Benoni. If this was the case, they would just have to start driving from one police station to another.

As they drove, Muzi told his worried babezala that he had set up a job interview for Tumelo that very morning, at half-past eleven, so they had no choice but to find him, and fast. And they would.

"I'm quite sure that Tshidi would have sent Tumelo a message to let him know about the interview," Muzi said.

By the time they drove past Germiston, the old man seemed to have sunk down further into his seat, unable to disguise his mounting worry. But the old man was also holding on to hope. "What would we do without you, *mkhwenyana* (son-in-law)? You are a blessing from above."

They eventually found Tumelo, two hours and three police stations later. Muzi happened to have a friend, a Captain Naidoo, who was a senior officer at the John Vorster precinct. Even though Tumelo was not being held at that station, Captain Naidoo made a few calls and established that the boy had been booked at the Hillbrow police station.

It was five o'clock in the morning when Muzi returned home. It had been a misunderstanding more than anything else. Or probably some Metro cops looking for a bribe. The police officers on duty that night had told Muzi that Tumelo had been rude and uncooperative when asked to produce his driver's licence. Tumelo said that he had explained to them that he had forgotten his driver's license at home in Daveyton, and then told them that he was driving his father's car. An argument had ensued, which led to a breathalyser test. Unfortunately for the young man, the test confirmed that he was slightly over the legal limit for alcohol, which had led to his arrest.

Fortunately, Captain Naidoo had already called ahead and pulled some rank, and the important thing was that the young man would not miss his interview. The way Muzi saw it, the mission had been accomplished, and that was all that mattered.

Muzi decided to see if he could fit in an hour's sleep. He set the alarm for a quarter past six and slid quietly into bed, trying not to wake Tshidi. She must have been wide-awake with worry while they were out looking for Tumelo, poor thing.

It was past seven o'clock when he felt Tshidi shaking him awake. He had not heard his alarm going off. He leapt out of bed, shouting to Tshidi that *yes everything was okay* and that *Tumelo was fine and wouldn't miss his interview*, all while throwing his pyjamas off and rushing into the shower. This was not a day to be running late. Not today. The client for today's pitch was too important.

As Muzi rushed out of the shower, he found Tshidi sitting up in bed, still asking questions about where and how they'd found Tumelo earlier on. He gave brief, staccato answers while hurriedly getting dressed.

"I can't be late my love, not today," he told her, slipping into a pair of Lanvin chinos and brown Florsheim brogues. He rushed over to the mirror to button up his crisp white shirt and then headed to the study to get his paperwork in order. Placing his laptop in the laptop bag, he searched frantically for his copy of the boardroom keys. Breathing a sigh of relief as he found them, he dashed towards the kitchen to tell Tshidi not to bother with breakfast; he would grab a coffee and a doughnut at the staff canteen.

But Tshidi was not in the kitchen.

He walked down the passage and into his daughter's bedroom hoping to find her there but found only Lethu, fast asleep in her cot.

Muzi turned back to the master bedroom and there, sitting in bed, texting on her phone, was his beautiful wife. She looked up at him. "What a night, hey baby?" she said, yawning, slowly getting up out of the bed.

"*Hawu, hhayi, hhayi, sthandwa sam,*" (No, no, my love) he said, suddenly feeling an unexpected surge of anger rising up inside him, "You mean to tell me all this time you didn't even think of making me a quick coffee? Couldn't you see that I was running late?"

Tshidi rolled her eyes at him and paused to put on her morning slippers. "Don't be so irritable," she laughed, "Chillax. What should I make you? Some eggs?"

But Muzi was already headed for the door. He was running late. What was the use of arguing anyway?

CHAPTER 3

He made it to work in the nick of time. Thankfully, the pitch went off without a hitch. In fact, it went off *far* better than 'without a hitch'. As he wrapped up his presentation, the clients were up on their feet, smiling, clapping for him, and patting him on the back. he could see that Darren, the Managing Director, was pleased with the way things had gone.

Back at his desk in the open plan office, Muzi took a moment to reflect on the morning. He thought back to his foolhardy attempt to nap for an hour after a night of driving around trying to get his youngest *sbali* out of jail. He thought about how he overslept after not hearing his phone's alarm go off; the hurried showering; the scrambling to get ready; his F1 driving exploits on the way to work; his nervousness before the pitch, and his relief afterwards. He'd had a crazy night and a crazy morning; there was no doubt about that.

Thank God the presentation had gone so well!

It was only then that Muzi realised, as he folded up his sleeves, that his shirt could have done with some ironing out. He usually hung his shirts up in the closet freshly ironed, so that in the mornings it was just a case of smoothing out a few light creases. He was particular about how his shirts were ironed, and much preferred doing it himself than leaving it to Tshidi or Lethu's nanny.

He always tried - and he and Tshidi were in agreement on this - to ensure that the nanny, a kind, frail, middle-aged woman they called *Ma Gumede*, was not burdened with any household work other than looking after the child. Lethu was a hyperactive toddler, and the poor woman had her hands full just keeping up with her. Anyway, the point was that today, his shirt was a little crumpled and Muzi, who was neat to a fault, noted this with dissatisfaction.

And Tshidi... Aargh, he had better stop thinking about how angry she had made him by the time he left the house. Perhaps she was right in thinking that he was being irritable. Lack of sleep can do that to one, no?

He suddenly felt the pangs of morning hunger. He was about to get up and head to the canteen when he felt a tap on his shoulder. He turned around. It was Tsakani, from Graphic Design.

"Looks like you had a rough morning mister," she said, smiling.

She placed a steaming styrofoam cup of coffee and a bagel on Muzi's desk.

"How did you know?" Muzi asked, pleasantly surprised and grateful. He stood up and gave her a hug.

Tsakani was a little on the short side, and a little on the plump side too, but she had a winsome smile and a heart of gold. She was, arguably, a six out of ten in the looks department, but often found herself warding off the advances of many a male colleague. Perhaps she was not attractive in the conventional sense of the word, but she more than made up for it with her beautiful personality. Something in her character, her manner, something undeniably feminine and effortlessly kind, made her attractive.

Not that Muzi thought of her in that way, of course. No, not as a romantic prospect. He was a married man, and he wasn't one of those married guys who identified as MBAs - married but available.

However, there was no denying - even though neither of them attempted to cross any boundaries - that Tsakani was drawn to him. She didn't pursue him or try to seduce him, but it often came through - slipped through - in an innocent and unassuming way, that she really did like him *in that way*.

"Some women are lucky," she had once said, in this very office, resulting in a few raised eyebrows. The conversation had been raging in the open plan space, and Muzi, unlike many of the other married men who worked there, had made it clear that he would never consider cheating on his wife.

The light-hearted banter in the ad agency often veered in the direction of relationships and 'the battle of the sexes'. Some of Muzi's colleagues had, on occasion, whispered to him about how they'd tried their luck with Tsakani and had been turned down. They were convinced it was because she had a serious crush on Muzi.

"Don't be silly," he would say every time the topic came up during guy-gossip at the office. *Hhayi*, he was always amazed at the way his male colleagues gossiped. Where had the idea that gossip was something that was mainly done by women come from? Had it ever been rooted in fact? Or was it just one of many things that were widely believed but untrue, like many other ideas that patriarchy had perpetrated with regard to women, in an attempt to make men seem superior?

If the idea that gossip was the province of women had begun as fact, Muzi was quite sure that it was no longer true in the present day. Everybody gossiped, and the men at this ad agency - it seemed to him - gossiped one hell of a lot.

But Muzi disliked the habit. He did not like talking about people behind their backs, and he usually responded to snippets of gossip with an uncomfortable smile and an awkward silence.

But back to the subject of Tsakani...

"Tsakani is not that kind of girl. She knows that I'm married," were Muzi's words when his colleagues teased him about her feelings towards him.

Some of the guys were somewhat more direct. "*Wabhay'za waitse, ngaona ole oa gobatla chief,*" (You're dumb, that girl wants you) Thabiso, the well-known Casanova from sales, would say, shaking his head. "If it was me I would have long tapped that, man." And Muzi did suspect, from the way she looked at him, that he could 'hit' if he really wanted to; if he really tried. There was 'that thing'; an attraction, between them, but it would never be explored because he wasn't about to cheat on his wife, even if Tshidi did make him angry sometimes.

Muzi thought about the events that had transpired at home earlier that morning. When had Tshidi become so inconsiderate? Had she changed? Or was he just being unreasonable? Was he being too sensitive? He was often plagued by the nagging thought that she wasn't trying hard enough to keep up with the added challenges of a parental and married life. But that thought usually ran parallel to many other competing thoughts in his mind, such as whether he was being sexist in his expectations. It was the last thing Muzi wanted to be, one of those old-fashioned men who was stuck in the old ways. He tried hard to break free from the *traditional* roles - sometimes disguised as Africanism - which had, historically, oppressed and even continued to oppress women in the present day.

But try as he might, his thoughts went back to that morning, and how completely unbothered Tshidi had been as he scrambled around, running late, anxious about his early morning presentation at work. What had made the situation worse was that the reason why he had hardly slept was because he had been looking for and getting *her* younger brother out of jail. How could she have been so insensitive? And why, whenever Muzi did try to bring up anything that was bothering him, was it always a case of "LOL," and "Moving right along."

Suddenly, without warning, a thought popped into his head and startled him.

"No man," Muzi hissed under his breath, annoyed with himself for thinking it. He had been comparing his wife's thoughtless behaviour that morning with Tsakani's recent *thoughtfulness*.

"No Muzi," he scolded himself, "You cannot start seeing her in that light. Stop thinking about her in that way. You're a married man for God's sake."

To be honest, he had realised, several months after Tsakani had joined the agency, endearing herself to everybody with her impeccable work ethic, her friendliness, and her all-around brilliance at her job, that this was a woman he might have pursued had he not been married. But the realisation was one he'd made without any sense of regret or longing. He had a beautiful wife - an absolutely stunning wife - whom he loved and cherished. And besides, the old saying was probably true, that the grass on the other side of the fence always looked greener than it really was. Tsakani was a good person; he had no reason to feel guilty for having noticed that. And the thought that if he wasn't married that she might have been someone that he would have pursued was nothing more than a passing thought; an honest thought with no ulterior motives.

Or was it?

He was still caught up in these thoughts when Tsakani happened to walk past his desk. He could smell her scent before he saw her. The earthy, sensuous fragrance announced her presence as she was about to breeze past, behind him. He guessed that it must have been her favourite perfume because she wore it many a time.

And then, from the corner of his eye, he would see her approaching silhouette. The moment always seemed to unravel in slow motion, leaving Muzi feeling unsettled and confused. The smell of her. The passing glance as she came into view behind him. The light pat on his shoulder. Was it a caress? Did it linger just a little longer than innocence would allow? And what about the reflexive way his hand would then shoot up to cover hers for a brief, sizzling moment? The tenderness in her voice when she said, "Hey you," before continuing on her way, a bundle of files clutched in the crook of her right arm?

A lump had formed in Muzi's throat. It was spontaneous, and it surprised him. He swallowed hard. He felt a sensation like a ball of ice settling in the pit of his stomach. He swivelled his chair around and his eyes locked on her booty, hugged tightly in a pair of designer jeans. Full. Shapely.

"Tsakani," Muzi heard himself call out, but the words came out barely above a whisper. The sound of his voice struck him as dry. Crackling. Somewhat strained. Tsakani stopped and turned around. She looked at him with kind, pretty, questioning eyes. Time insisted on drawing the moment out in slow motion.

"I, um, I meant to ask how far you guys are with the graphics for the beverage company? The energy drink one." This is what Muzi's lips said. But his heart – which thankfully, she could not see - said something else. If she could, she would hear it saying, "Tsakani, you are incredible,"

In the flash of that instant, frozen in a moment of time, he saw the look in Tsakani's eyes turn from curious to – suddenly - shy.

Muzi seemed to look down at the exact moment as Tsakani, and she seemed to look up at the exact moment when he looked up again. Their eyes met for a nanosecond, and in that highly charged instant, something passed between them. Something silent and unspoken. Could it have been recognition? Or acceptance? Whatever it may have been, it was something that would change things between them forever, whether they would ever act on it or not. It was a moment of mutual and effortless acknowledgement.

Mumbling, Tsakani said that she'd update him on how far graphics were with the visuals he was asking about later that afternoon, and then turned around and carried on to wherever she'd been going.

Muzi looked around, feeling self-conscious, almost certain that their workmates in the office must have seen, or felt, the electric current that had just passed between them. But his embarrassment was misplaced. There was no need to worry. All around him, his colleagues were either hunched over their computers or caught up in small talk.

Only he and Tsakani knew that something had just happened between them. He had felt something, and he knew that she had felt it too. Yes, definitely, *something*, even if it did not have a name or found no expression in action or words; even if it never led to anything for as long as they lived. Something *had* passed between them. And it was something that he had no business experiencing or feeling.

Lunchtime came and went and, though they tried to avoid each other, their eyes kept meeting. Randomly. Indecently. "What the heck is wrong with you, man?" Muzi thought. He wondered if he was the only one who was caught up in this sudden burst of hormones. What if Tsakani was just being her usual warm, friendly self? Would that be a good thing or a bad thing?

Muzi tried immersing himself in his work, but he could not focus. He couldn't wait for knocking-off time. He wanted to go home. Home to his beautiful wife and his adorable daughter. Home, away from the confusing feelings that were causing him so much stress.

It was a quarter to three. Muzi decided to go down to the basement and chill in his car for a while. He had to pull himself together.

Muzi and all the other mid-management creatives worked on the first floor of a five-storey building. His preferred parking space was on B1, just below the ground floor. He decided to take the stairs; he'd bump into fewer people that way. Down on the ground floor, he began descending the last flight of steps, and then he paused. It was that fragrance again.

There, just one step up from the foot of the stairs, was Tsakani, walking up from B1. It was a narrow stairwell. She looked up and, seeing him, took a step down to allow him to pass. Muzi descended the few steps that separated them. It would be difficult to determine who kissed whom first. Instantly, effortlessly, they were in each other's arms. They were kissing, eyes shut tight in the magic of the moment. Muzi's head was spinning. Her lips were so soft, so sweet. His tongue probed. His hands cupped her firm buttocks. He was crazy with desire.

They must both have heard the door to the stairway, one floor up, swing open because they seemed to disengage at the same time. Not a word was spoken, but Muzi thought, in the flash of a fleeting look, that he could see tears in Tsakani's eyes. He walked towards his car. Tsakani began walking back up the stairwell.

No words had been spoken. No words were necessary.

CHAPTER 4

Returning to his office forty-five minutes later, Muzi was angry with himself. He was stunned by the stupidity and recklessness of his encounter with Tsakani. He loved being married. He loved his family. Tshidi was the love of his life, dammit. So what if Tsakani was such a wonderful person? *So what!* There was no way he could ever feel for Tsakani what he felt for Tshidi. He loved Tshidi. My God, he loved his wife! What was this nonsense that was going on with him? Kissing a woman at work, in a deserted stairwell?

Whatever was going on with him, Muzi decided that it could not continue. He would make sure of it. He simply could not do this to his family, Muzi thought, his lips pursed with determination "Tshidi and Lethu are my life!" He was busy thinking in exclamation marks, convincing himself...

He spent the last hour of his day at work buying stuff online for his wife and daughter, and calling various business and social contacts, arranging favours and surprises for his in-laws. He bought perfume and expensive lingerie for Tshidi, and a cute tricycle for his daughter. He wangled two VIP tickets to a Stimela concert from his events-organiser friend, Jack. He would be gifting these tickets to his father-in-law, a staunch fan of the Afro-fusion band. Muzi was certain that the old man would be thrilled with the show, and the fact that the tickets were VIP was an added bonus. He wondered if he was trying to assuage his guilt over kissing Tsakani in the stairwell, but the truth was that he was not. He was just being his usual self. Generous. Giving. It felt good to do stuff for his family and his in-laws.

By the time Muzi left the office early that evening, he felt that he'd reminded himself of what made him happy. What was important to him was family, not workplace flings. God forbid!

Tomorrow, he would tell Tsakani that what had happened on the stairwell could not happen again. He would tell her that he would never leave his wife and that he was not about to have an affair behind her back either. No. He just didn't roll like that. *"I'm a responsible, loving, faithful family man,"* Muzi reminded himself. *"I'm not a player. This whole thing is just so ridiculous, so unlike me"* he thought, reclaiming his sanity. *"It had been a moment of weakness, yes, but that was all it was going to be. Nothing more. Just a moment of madness."*

Back home, Muzi enjoyed a beautiful evening with his wife and daughter.

"Wow, someone is really in a good mood! Is it thank-God-it's-Friday things or what?" Tshidi teased him, as he lavished her and Lethu with affection.

"Hhayibo, I'm just being my normal loving self," Muzi shot back, laughing.

Tshidi seemed to think about this for a minute, screwing up her face jokingly as she did. *"Hmmmn, nna ne ke nagana gore* (you know, I thought) you were angry with me when you left this morning, baby," she said.

"Nah sweetheart, I was just running late, that's all my love," Muzi told her, freeing one of his hands from holding Lethu, whose head was nestling on his shoulder, to grab Tshidi by the waist and pull her in for a kiss.

The following day was one of Tshidi's stokvel[5] days, and Muzi spent the latter part of his Friday evening making sure that everything was prepared and ready.

Whenever Tshidi's crew came over for one of their girls'-get-togethers, Muzi always played the role of designated braai[6] master. On the way home from work, he had already passed by his favourite butcher to stock up on meat and boerewors.

He busied himself, ensuring that the meat was properly marinated. He would leave it to soak in the succulent flavours overnight, and by the time he put it

---

[5] An invitation only club

[6] A South African term for grilling meat over an open fire

on the fire around noontime on Saturday, the meat would be juicy and as tasty as hell.

He had also stopped by the bottle store to stock up on the wines and ciders that Tshidi and her girls liked to drink during their stokvels.

Muzi's role was to make sure everything was provided for and prepared, and it was a role that he was always ready to perform. His preparation routine involved checking the standby fridge in the garage, making sure that he took out the ice buckets in the corner for the following days' guests, and ensuring that he had enough charcoal for the braai.

Muzi would usually invite one or two friends over to keep him company while he braaied for Tshidi's crew and made sure everything went off without any problems.

At around half past eight that evening, Muzi's cell phone rang. It was his childhood friend, Musa. "I've got two luxury suite tickets for the derby tomorrow," Musa said, "You interested bru? *As'bangene*" (Let's go).

Muzi remembered that it was a Pirates-versus-Chiefs weekend. Soccer City would be packed. Under normal circumstances, Muzi would have taken up the offer in a heartbeat; Soweto derbies were a highlight of any season; but instead, he convinced Musa to come over and help him with the following day's braaing. He also managed to convince Musa to come through the following morning and hand over the tickets so that he could give them to his *sbali* Lehlogonolo, Tshidi's eldest brother, who lived close by.

Lehlogonolo was over the moon with excitement when Muzi called to tell him about the tickets and excitedly promised to come and fetch them first thing in the morning. "Not so fast, *sbali*," Muzi said, calming the die-hard Pirates supporter down, "Musa is only bringing the tickets over after ten. Come through any time after eleven."

Joining Tshidi and Lethu in the lounge after he had finished marinating the meat, he told Tshidi about the derby tickets he had just arranged for her brother. She laughed and said he spoilt her brothers way too much. But he knew she was grateful.

"You've got such a giving nature, my baby," she said, clasping his hand in hers as he sat down on the sofa beside her, while Lethu caused chaos on the living room floor; trying to play with dozens of toys all at once.

While they watched TV, Tshidi told him about her latest business idea. Muzi attempted to listen with as much enthusiasm as he could muster, given his wife's record of business schemes. They usually involved the buying and selling of expensive women's products or accessories, and they all invariably ended with considerable money being spent, not much money being made, and unsold stock sitting idly in the garage. Either that or she would give her top-selling merchandise out on credit to customers who never paid.

The excitement with which Tshidi usually embarked on these little side hustles of hers was always quite contagious. She was always convinced that she was going make a killing, but without fail, money would be spent that could not be recovered.

So the latest business idea was designer handbags. *Eish.* Muzi wanted to ask detailed questions about where she would get her stock, how she would price the bags, and who her client base would be, but instead he decided to sit back and simply listen as she spoke about how much money they'd be rolling in if she could just get the right stock in the right quantities.

Tshidi wasn't a small-scale *test-the-market-first* kind of thinker. In that moment, she was trying to convince him that she needed to start off with at least thirty bags, and she was energetically showing him pictures of the designer handbags on her phone. It was all rather exclusive and very costly merchandise as far as he could tell - Prada and Louis Vuitton and the like. He would have to convince her to bring the number down significantly. A whole thirty to begin with? There was no way that he was spending that kind of money on initial stock; not with Tshidi's dismal record in selling stuff.

But tonight, he just listened attentively and patiently as she went on about how much money she would make this time. He would give his input another time. Not tonight. These schemes of hers always ended up costing them dearly, especially once her initial excitement subsided.

Muzi woke up feeling like a new man that Saturday morning. The week had taken its toll on him, both physically and emotionally, and he'd fallen asleep to the vague sound of Tshidi talking excitedly to one friend after another about the stokvel that she was hosting the following day. He'd slept like a baby, except for some time around half past three in the morning when he had to go and see to Lethu, who was screaming in the next room.

The toddler was developing a strategy for these nocturnal cries for attention, Muzi thought. She no longer cried non-stop until one of her parents came to calm and/or feed her. Not anymore. She had taken to yell-cries where she paused just long enough to let out an even louder yelp if no one appeared at her bedside.

Every little change in her growth and behaviour fascinated and amused Muzi, the doting father that he was. He would often wonder, as he rocked her back to sleep, about the English referring to deep sleep as "sleeping like a baby". Whoever had come up with that expression was clearly clueless about the sleeping habits of babies.

It was a bright Saturday morning and Muzi was in a good mood. When he stepped outside to breathe in some of the crisp early-morning air, the clear blue sky streaked above him in a never-ending expanse of azure magic. He was looking forward to seeing Musa, who he'd organised to be his braai buddy for the day. They would chat about old times and knock back a few cold ones while making sure that Tshidi and her stokvel crew were fed perfectly braaied meat.

Musa was still one of the funniest guys Muzi knew, and one of a very small circle of people that Muzi counted on as his close friends. He enjoyed catching up with his friends in the relaxed environment of his own home. Although he went out with the boys every now and then, he always made sure that he left when the guys felt like the night was beginning to *warm up*. "The 8pm man," they would call him, always trying to get him to hang out a little longer. But Muzi was resolute, despite the casual teasing and taunting. The thought of his wife and little daughter alone in the house late at night didn't sit well with him, even though he had installed a state-of-the-art security system to make his home inaccessible to those who broke into houses in the still of the night. As a husband and a father, Muzi took his roles as provider and protector seriously. "Some of us have families to see to," Muzi would always say, reaching for his phone and immobiliser, and side-eyeing some of the married guys and fathers that he was leaving behind.

CHAPTER 5

After setting up his braai stand, Muzi sat down on his favourite Eazi-Chair on the patio at the back the house. Phone in hand, he began to compose a Whatsapp message to Tsakani. He felt that enough time had passed since their spontaneous, troubling embrace in the stairwell. He was inclined to take a rather pragmatic view of the encounter now, instead of merely wallowing in his feelings of guilt. What had happened had happened, but it would not happen again. It *could not* happen again.

His typed message was not too long, but not too short either. His words were formal and somewhat stiff; the message of a man trying to distance himself in the eyes of someone with whom he'd had an inappropriately close encounter.

Hello Tsakani,

*I thought I should just clear the air about what
happened between us at work yesterday. I am sorry that
I put you in the position that I did. I was out of line.
You know how much my family means to me. I have no
intention of doing anything that would cause emotional
harm to my wife and my daughter. You are a wonderful
person, and I have no doubt that your soul mate is out
there looking for you. I hope that we can still be friends
and that we will still be able to work well together.*

Muzi

He read it through once and sent it. *You are doing the
right thing,* his head said. *Are you sure? Completely sure?*
his heart asked. Muzi chuckled and remembered a
favourite verse of ubaba'Ncane, the man who had
raised him. He couldn't say exactly where it had been
said, or exactly *what* it said - it had been so long since
he'd read from the Bible - but he knew that it was
somewhere in the book of Jeremiah, in the Old
Testament. It said something about the human heart
being very, very deceitful, above all else. That verse

- 43 -

made sense to him, as he grew older. Common sense and responsibility should guide a man during those times when his heart tried to lead him astray.

The weather remained perfect for the remainder of the day, and everything went according to plan. Musa arrived just after ten, and not long after eleven o'clock Tshidi's brother Lehlogonolo arrived to collect the derby tickets that Musa had sacrificed in order to spend the day at Muzi's place.

Just after noon, with the braai fire already lit and the coals beginning to sizzle, Muzi and Musa took a short drive to a nearby supermarket that stocked fresh salmon. When they returned, Muzi wrapped the fish in foil and set it down around the edges of the fire. By late afternoon, it would serve as an after-lunch snack for Tshidi's friends; the ladies of the stokvel.

Tshidi's stokvel days were the only time that two-year-old Lethu didn't follow her dad around. The ladies were too busy spoiling her and showering her with attention for her to be bothered about him. Muzi and Musa passed the time braaing, taking the meat that was ready indoors, chatting about old times, and knocking back some beers. Even though Musa was his best friend, Muzi didn't tell him about the kissing incident with Tsakani. It was not that he hadn't thought about mentioning it to his friend, because he had, but when the thought arose, he quickly dismissed it. He preferred to think about it as being something that wasn't too deep.

In any case, it wouldn't happen again.

At game time, which was around 3pm, after Musa and Muzi had shared a plate of delicious salmon, having taken the rest into the kitchen, the friends took a drive to Sabza's house to watch the Pirates versus Chiefs derby, and have a few drinks. Sabza was a mutual friend who lived nearby, and he, unlike his two die-hard Pirates supporter friends, was a Chiefs fan. "I want you guys to come and watch at my place so I can laugh at you *kahle mase sinithele induku* (when we've thrashed you)," he said earlier that day when he called to invite them over.

But the match did not live up to expectations, ending in a goalless draw, just like every other Soweto Derby league encounter that had taken place in the last few years. Nobody could laugh at anybody, and they spent the hour after the game quaffing beers and lamenting the state of the country's largest football derby.

By the time Muzi returned home shortly before eight that night, Lethu had had enough of all the doting, noisy aunties in the house and she just wanted to be with her daddy. She fell asleep in his arms, exhausted, within a few minutes of his arrival, and he put her to bed.

As Muzi walked into his study, he noticed that he had a Whatsapp message on his phone. It was from Tsakani. Muzi took a seat on the two-seater couch that was positioned just inside the doorway and opened the message.

He was hopeful that she would not be too upset with him, even though, by all rights, she probably should have been, especially considering that no matter what she said or felt, he was not going to be changing his mind. He was not having this affair. Not this one, nor any affair, for that matter. He was choosing to remain true to his marriage vows.

The phone hung limply in his hand as he tried to collect his emotions. He stared up at the ceiling and sighed deeply. Tsakani was not about to make this easy for him.

Muzi darling,

Yes, I know that I have no right to call you that, but I might as well tell you, just this once, how I feel. After that, I will leave you alone.

Muzi, ever since the day I met you, I've had the hots for you. I haven't always admitted it to myself because of course, I knew that I had no right to. But in my heart I knew.

I am SO into you, Muzi. But, I want nothing but happiness for you. I would never do anything if I thought that it would hurt you. Yes, you have a friend in me and I will be the same professional, courteous colleague at work that you know me to be. But always know how I feel about you.

I can't help how I feel. I respect your wishes, I know you are married. It makes no sense to me that my heart feels this way. Imma leave you alone because I would do anything for you and that's what you want me to do.

Tsakani

He chided himself for his conflicting feelings. His heart was thumping loudly in his throat. He assured himself that it was because of Tsakani's pain, which came out so clearly in her text message, squashing any thoughts that it was also, partly, his own pain. The chapter was closed before it had begun, and correctly so; he was a married man. A married, *committed, faithful* man.

Muzi went to check in on Lethu, to see if she hadn't woken up from the ever-growing din generated by the voices and laughter of Tshidi's stokvel gathering. But she was fast asleep with her thumb in her mouth; her latest sleeping position.

He went over to the noisy living room with its open sliding glass doors leading out onto a raised patio of cobbled stone. After graciously appreciating all the compliments about his recent renovations to the house - and of course his famous braaing skills - Muzi bid his house guests goodnight, kissed Tshidi self-consciously as the crew serenaded them, and headed off to take a shower.

Tshidi would be more than a little tipsy by the time she came to bed, and she had told him the night before, with a naughty twinkle in her eyes, that she "was gonna light his fire" come Saturday night. Muzi was breathless with anticipation. It had been a while since he'd had mind-blowing sex with his beautiful wife. Their sex life had, in fact, almost become extinct, somewhat like the rhino, whose horn our brothers in the East swear is a *mvusankunzi* (aphrodisiac).

Muzi lay in bed smiling at the contrasting images in his thoughts. He was a little sleepy, but looking forward to a night of passionate lovemaking.

After Tshidi's guest had left, Muzi set about making sure that everything was well secured; that every alarm was activated, and every security gate was locked. One couldn't be careful enough. House burglaries constituted a major part of violent crimes committed nationally and had been on the rise in their neighbourhood every year since they'd bought their house.

Walking back into the bedroom, Muzi disrobed and jumped into bed under the covers beside Tshidi, butt naked and rock hard. But Tshidi was fast asleep; no sooner had her head hit the pillow. She drowsily put off his expectant caresses, squashing any chance of them making love. "*Hhawu Tshidi, nanamuhla ngishay'wa isandla,*" (Even tonight you're pushing me away) Muzi whispered, but she was already snoring softly.

The following morning, after he'd prepared his wife a greasy, meaty, chilli breakfast to deal with her hangover, making enough for her to share with her two close friends who had slept over, Muzi attempted to get some work done in the study. Tshidi had taken a blanket and headed to the guest bedroom, and he knew the women would be holed up in the room, gossiping and laughing for the rest of the day. Lethu was in there too.

The day was overcast and a little on the cold side. Sitting in his study, unable to concentrate, Muzi mused that the weather seemed to match his mood, although he couldn't quite pinpoint the reason why. It was obvious to him that he couldn't, and wouldn't be getting any work done.

Good-natured laughter rang out from a few rooms away; his wife and her friends were happy, but Muzi, somehow, was incomprehensibly unhappy.

Muzi had his phone in his hand when Tsakani's incoming WhatsApp message vibrated and flashed on his screen. He opened it, but there were no words to read. Instead, a series of red and pink hearts fluttered across the screen, with a kiss emoji rounding them off.

He was unsure of how to reply to her, but it was becoming clearer to Muzi that he needed to deal with the Tsakani situation once and for all. He might be going through a rough patch in his marriage, but this dry spell didn't mean that he loved Tshidi any less. In a rather confusing way, the fact that there were problems between him and his wife made it even clearer now - in that particular moment - that he needed to decisively finish this *thing* that had begun starting with Tsakani and focus on getting his marriage back on track.

With this thought in mind, Muzi quickly texted Tsakani back and asked her to send him directions to her place. He didn't want to have an ongoing WhatsApp conversation with her about where they stood and felt it would be more impactful if he told her in person that they couldn't pursue whatever it was that was brewing between them. The face-to-face confrontation would ensure that Tsakani physically *saw* his determination to respect his marriage vows.

Leaving the house was easy and didn't require any covering up. He simply told Tshidi, who was caught up in gossip and raucous laughter with her friends, that he had to go and see "someone".

The guest bedroom was jam-packed; five women on the bed and sleeper couches, curing their babalas[7] and laughing and gossiping loudly. Three more of Tshidi's friends had arrived, ostensibly to collect a casserole dish that one of them had brought along the previous afternoon, but actually because this was their usual routine for their stokvel weekend Sunday mornings.

Tshidi offered Muzi a cheek to kiss and, before he could rethink his steps, he was out on the road, driving to an address on the other side of Benoni, in Lakeview, where Tsakani lived.

The first thing he noticed about the décor in her apartment was that it reminded him, in the artistic minimalism of it all; of a townhouse he'd furnished himself during his bachelor days. They shared a similar taste, he thought to himself.

Muzi was suddenly overcome with a feeling of guilt for being there, in her apartment. *"What are you doing?"* he questioned himself silently, the voice in his head steadily growing in volume from a whisper to a roar.

---

[7] A South African word for a hangover

He started making small talk, but Tsakani took the initiative and moved towards him. She enveloped him in a tight hug and began to kiss him. Muzi's head was spinning. He felt the softness of her lips, the hunger in her probing tongue, and the passion in her tight embrace. The question in his mind was screaming now. *"What are you doing?!"*

Muzi pulled away from her, muttering something incoherent about how he couldn't do this. He started toward the door in a blind panic. He could not allow himself to break his marriage vows, not even with someone as wonderful and as incredible as Tsakani.

The last thing Muzi heard on his way out of the door - fleeing the scene of his infidelity - was Tsakani's voice, twisted into a desperate plea. "Muzi! Don't go! Please don't go! Muzi! I love you!"

But Muzi was already determined to leave. He was not going to do this. Not to his wife, not to his family, and certainly not to himself.

CHAPTER 6

Muzi arrived back at the house having driven like a lunatic. He was visibly shaken. He knew that he needed to find a way to put an end to this thing that was brewing between him and Tsakani, once and for all. But how?

But while preparing a late lunch for Tshidi and her remaining visitors, warming up some of the sumptuous meats and fish he'd braaied the day before, it became clearer to him what he needed to do. He would Whatsapp her and explain to her that it had been a mistake for them to even kiss. He would tell her that she deserved so much more than being a married man's side chick. He would remind her — once again - that there was somebody out there who deserved her love. He would — once again - make it clear that his family was his most important reason for living, and he could not betray his vows or desert his responsibilities simply because he wanted to have an affair. His family didn't deserve that. *Tsakani* didn't deserve that. He could not go through with such selfish behaviour. Yes, he wanted her badly - he would not lie about his feelings - but this situation required his principles to override his emotions.

He could hear the voices of Tshidi and her friends from the guest bedroom. He could also hear the delighted peals of laughter as Lethu enjoyed the attention of a room full of women. These sounds of happiness were proof that the family he worked so hard for was content. He would not rock that boat, not even for a woman as remarkable as Tsakani. He simply couldn't, and he wouldn't do it.

Later that evening, with all the guests having left, and Lethu safely tucked up in bed and fast asleep, Muzi walked into the main bedroom with one thought on his mind; he wanted to make love to his beautiful wife.

But one look at Tshidi made it clear that this wasn't going to happen. She was in that deep sleep that accompanies spending an entire day 'curing' a hangover with further drinking. Muzi got into bed and tried to fall asleep, but he found himself tossing and turning. Beside him, Tshidi snored softly, having practically blacked out from the weekend's drinking. He knew that he would need to sit down with her at some point and talk about the things that made him feel like his needs were being neglected in their marriage.

Back at work that Monday proved to be awkward for both Muzi and Tsakani. Muzi had arrived early at the office that morning and had sent her a long email. She had clearly read it. They spent most of the day trying to avoid each other. Perhaps there was nothing more to be said.

Their eyes met during their tea break. Tsakani was embroiled in a loud discussion with a group of mostly women over what everyone would be doing for the upcoming Christmas break. Muzi was eavesdropping when Tsakani said that she always spent Christmas holidays with her in-laws, the family of her eldest sister's husband. She spoke about how she envied her sisters - all of whom were married - and how they got a chance to play the role of *makoti*[8] every Christmas and on other long holiday breaks.

"Hayi, shem me (poor me), if I ever get married, I'm gonna look forward to every chance I get to serve my in-laws and make them feel appreciated," she said, and added, "I'm gonna be so extra." It was at that point that Muzi looked up at her and caught her eye. She was looking directly at him. Was she trying to tell him something, he wondered? Reading her expression, Muzi saw more sadness than anger.

Her words left Muzi thinking about something else that he needed to address with Tshidi. There were constant arguments whenever holiday season came around and Muzi wanted to take the family to Witbank, where most of his biological father's family lived.

---

[8] A South African word for a bride; a newly-wed woman; or a daughter-in-law.

While Muzi pointed out that she only had to visit her in-laws once or, at the most, twice a year, and reminded her that *he* spent the rest of the year being of service and assistance to *her* family, she saw no value in spending time with his family.

Tshidi would always complain about having to go there; not that there was much work to do - because Tshidi was treated with great consideration by her in-laws and was not expected to serve them from dawn to dusk, or wear the customary *doek*[9] like many makotis in Black families were expected to do.

But Tshidi grumbled that she didn't have a close relationship with any of his relatives and that she didn't have any friends in Witbank.

She complained that she became bored and lonely when Muzi spent time reconnecting with old childhood friends and acquaintances during those holiday visits. "But Tshidi, have you *tried* to make friends with any of my relatives?" Muzi would usually counter when Tshidi started complaining about

---

[9] A South African word for a headscarf

having to spend the holidays *ekhabo Muzi*[10], "It won't just happen magically; you're going to have to put some effort into it."

She would also argue that being in Witbank with his family meant that she had no privacy, no time alone to herself to do as she pleased or take a drive somewhere with her daughter.

"But it's only once a year, Tshidi," Muzi would shoot back, "Is that too much of a sacrifice to make? You are being selfish." But Tshidi would hear nothing of it. The arguments would usually end with Tshidi in tears, Muzi apologising, and Tshidi getting her way.

After a few years, Muzi stopped pushing the issue and they would end up spending Christmas and New Year with Tshidi's family in Daveyton. If only Tshidi could be a bit more like Tsakani when it came to such things, Muzi thought, wistfully.

The ad agency had decided that they would have their annual staff party that Thursday; their last day of

---

[10] At Muzi's place

work before the company closed for their Christmas break.

The tension between Muzi and Tsakani had begun to subside as the days dragged slowly on. She had replied to his WhatsApp message that Tuesday, and it was perhaps the tone of that reply that had made things easier between them. There was no bitterness that laced the words that came with her reply. She didn't come across as a woman scorned. She seemed to accept Muzi's decision to put an end to their fledgling romance with grace and acceptance.

Muzi, my love,

I spent the whole night thinking about whether it was necessary for me to reply to your email. I decided that I should, just to clear the air between us. I need you to know and understand that I respect your decision, and I don't hate you for cutting me off. Thank you for encouraging me with your words about how you are sure that there is someone out there for me with whom I too can build a family. I don't know if that will happen, but thank you for trying to reassure me.

What I do know is that I love you like I have never loved a man before and that I will never stop loving you. No matter what happens or doesn't happen, always know that.

That I love you, always and forever.

Yours, Tsakani

After this message, Tsakani became her old sweet, caring, friendly self again towards him, and he felt himself beginning to relax again around her.

On the home front, however, things were not as rosy.

Tshidi's last day of work was that same Tuesday, and there were constant arguments between the couple over her attitude towards the chores that needed to be done around the house, despite the fact that *Ma Gumede* continued to come in every day to help with minding Lethu.

Muzi was growing increasingly impatient with her casual approach to carrying out basic tasks. He would find her watching TV or busy on her phone, with dinner not yet prepared. If he seemed to be running late in the mornings, she would lie in bed watching him scramble around; not offering to help with anything. When they were not arguing, there were long, deafening silences between them that would go on for hours.

There was a great deal of excitement about the impending break from work, and quite a bit of drinking going on at the Christmas party that Thursday night. It had been a good year for business, moreover, and everyone was overjoyed to have received their Christmas bonuses. Muzi had planned to leave at around half past seven, never one to break his eight o'clock rule about getting home, Christmas party or no Christmas party.

He had left the party to visit the men's bathroom. Standing at the basin washing his hands, the door of one of the sit-down toilets behind him swung open and Tsakani, embarrassed that she had strayed into the gents facility, appeared coyly from inside.

"Hey you," Muzi said as she walked towards him.

Both tipsy from the festivities, and before either one of them could say another word, caution was thrown to the wind and they were in each other's arms, kissing passionately. Risking one of their colleagues walking in on their breathless, urgent kissing, Tsakani was the first to pull away. She was not even supposed to be in men's toilets to begin with.

She giggled nervously, blushing, and made for the exit. Muzi attempted to pull her back towards him for another embrace, quite beside himself with wanting her.

"Wait, baby, not here," she said, her own voice choking with desire, "Meet me in the boardroom upstairs in thirty minutes, she said, breathlessly, "Nobody will disturb us there. I'll be waiting."

And with that, she was gone.

CHAPTER 7

Muzi watched Tsakani from the corner of his eye, all the while pretending to be engrossed in the loud, joyous, and somewhat drunken banter that surrounded them in the conference room. Alcoholic drinks flowed freely and the party was in full swing.

After telling some of her colleagues that she needed some air and had probably "had too much to drink", Tsakani slipped out of the room. Muzi watched her leave. Not wanting to arouse suspicion, he waited a few minutes before he too slipped away. It was unlikely, however, that anybody would have noticed anything.

Arriving at the boardroom, Muzi found the door slightly ajar. The lights were off. He stepped inside and Tsakani motioned to him to close the door behind him. Her key was dangling from the inside keyhole. Muzi quickly locked it. Turning around, he found Tsakani taking off her top, revealing her ample bosom of cream-coloured breasts, as full as watermelons, spilling out of her brown brassiere. The mere sight of her drove him wild with desire.

He took her swiftly into his arms and they began to kiss, their tongues teasing, probing and mingling with the other. Her hands trailed up the sides of his arms, and he felt her fingers playing with his earlobes, darting tantalisingly in and out of the caverns in his ears and making his entire body tingle. Her hands tugged at his belt, loosening it, unbuttoning and unzipping him until his pants fell to the floor.

She was kneeling down in front of him. Muzi was as hard as a rock, her tongue and fingers had left a trail of heat burning over every inch of his skin. She pulled his boxer shorts down and, like a magician, whipped out a condom and began wrapping it over his huge erection. She took his throbbing manhood into her mouth. A pale light filtered into the room from the adjoining passage, and Muzi watched her luscious lips clamping on and sucking and teasing the tip of his penis with the tip of her tongue. It took a great deal of effort for Muzi not to start moaning loudly. He grabbed at her afro and pulled her face further in, plunging himself deep into her throat, a climax ready to explode from his every pore.

She seemed to sense that he was on the verge of coming because she pulled her lips slowly over the shaft of his stiff erection and began to tease his head with her tongue, caressing him, teasing him, bringing him closer to and then pulling him away from the point of no return. Muzi was in agony and ecstasy. She turned to look up at him and once again brought him to the brink of an explosion.

Tsakani's left hand was extended upwards, her nails scraping lightly over his nipples, alternating from one side to the other, sending shivers of ecstasy shooting through his body. Tugging at her hair, quite mad and grimacing in the pleasure of the moment, Tsakani made him come like a river bursting its banks, one hand manoeuvring back and forth over his shaft while her lips seemed to drain every last bit of cream from the inner channels of his manhood.

Muzi was weak in the knees as he pulled up his boxer shorts and trousers, leaning against the polished wood of the imposing mahogany boardroom table. Tsakani briskly put on her blouse and extracted a tissue from her handbag; wrapping it around the used, sagging condom.

Both fully dressed, they held each other in a long, tight embrace. "I don't think I've had a blowjob like that before," Muzi whispered in Tsakani's ear, kissing her on the mouth, marvelling at the tenderness of her lips. She smiled, her eyes gleaming in the dark. Standing on her tiptoes, she brought her mouth to his once more.

"Well, I don't think I've seen anyone pump a condom so full of cum that it overflows," she replied. They both giggled.

"You are a beautiful man, Muzi. I'm here anytime you want to feel like that again," she said, and then added, "I'm *so* into you." They embraced once more, tightly, hungrily. "I'm into you too, baby," Muzi replied, his breathing laboured.

She stepped away from him, removing her key from the door. Her voice was a hushed whisper now. "Remember to use your own key to lock, my love. And only follow me after five minutes," she said.

She leaned in to give him one last kiss and then exited the boardroom.

Muzi sat there in the dark, feeling spent but energised all at the same time. Without settling the matter in his head, he knew that the only way to keep himself from having a full-blown affair with Tsakani would be if she herself decided to put an end to it. And he knew that she wouldn't do that. She loved him. She wanted him. And she made him feel wanted; a feeling he hadn't enjoyed in his marriage for quite some time.

Thinking about it, Muzi could not remember feeling wanted by Tshidi since Lethu's birth. He realised that his marriage had been in trouble for a while now. He could, therefore, hardly place the full blame on Tsakani for being such a loving, giving, and incredibly irresistible woman. Nor could he completely blame himself for having fallen for her. If anything, Muzi felt like his wife had made it easy for him to end up having an affair. Why was it that she could take, and take, and take, and yet never feel like giving? Tsakani was the polar opposite. He thought about their recent – and first - sexual encounter, where she had taken pleasure only in the act of giving him pleasure. Her every touch and her every kiss had set his body on fire.

Caught up in these thoughts, trying to make sense out of how he had become the very thing he so despised – an MBA - it was more than five minutes that had passed when Muzi eventually left the boardroom, locking up behind him and heading back to the party. He was conscious of the fact that his knees were wobbly. What a blowjob that had been!

He could not get Tsakani off his mind that night.

The following day, Muzi had every excuse for leaving the house, despite the fact that it was the company's Christmas break. He told Tshidi that he was "tying up some loose ends at the office." Knowing how conscientious he was about his job, there was no reason for her suspicion to be provoked. Muzi had, shortly after waking up, already texted Tsakani, telling her that he was heading over to her place.

"I can't wait to see you," was all she texted back.

When he arrived at her apartment, they kissed and held each other tight. Tsakani invited him to take a seat in her artistically furnished lounge. As he made himself comfortable, she emerging from her kitchen with a tray. A chilli breakfast with bacon and a tender steak and eggs, and a Bloody Mary in a tall glass.

"Welcome to T's famous hangover cure," she said, setting the tray down in front of him, finishing it off with a respectful curtsey that surprised him. He had certainly never been served like this in his own home.

She removed a vinyl from its sleeve and placed it on the vinyl player next to her huge bookshelf, disappearing into her bedroom. It was Sade; Tsakani was a jazzophile just as he was, he thought.

As Muzi drained the last of his Bloody Mary, feeling like the breakfast and liquid cure had dealt thoroughly with his hangover, he looked up to see Tsakani doing the catwalk towards him, wearing nothing but tiny slips of red and black lingerie. Her lips were moulded into a sexy pout, and her eyes had a *Come Duze* [11]look in them that immediately made Muzi grow hard; inflamed with desire; wanting her.

Positioning herself on the leather recliner, Tsakani straddled herself over Muzi and began to undress him. She gently pushed him down as he attempted to lift his head, her nails finding his nipples and igniting an electric current of arousal that coursed through his body. Keeping his eyes open was near impossible; the pleasure of her touch, the skilful and deliberate way in which she touched him had him seeing stars. She stripped him naked while playing with his hotspots, teasing him into a frenzy of heat and passion.

Tsakani removed her racy lingerie and, again, whipped a condom out of nowhere. Her fingers expertly rolled it down over the tip of his throbbing

---

[11] *Come closer, baby*

shaft. Their eyes were locked together. She placed him at the wet entrance of her burning bush and began to slowly ease him inside her. The intensity of the moment was incomprehensive for both of them. Eyes closed, bucking and leaping on top of Muzi, her lips parted like the lips of her labia that had his cock enveloped in their tight grasp, Tsakani began to ride him. It was as if her labia had a life of their own, Muzi thought, like fingers that knew exactly how to hold and stroke and squeeze and tease his rock hard shaft. Their sheer length and tight elasticity had him wondering whether what he had heard about Tsonga women was not a baseless rumour after all.

Deep thrusts alternated with playful dalliances. She raised her body off his slightly, allowing only the tip of his cock to remain inside her. She was moaning out his name while changing the depth of her downward thrust in ways that brought him to the verge of exploding, only to pull him back from the brink again.

She changed position now, squatting over him, and the deep penetration made them both gasp. They were moaning each other's names and Muzi watched

Tsakani's face shimmer with tiny droplets of sweat as she rode him. It was a call and response chorus of ecstasy that was beginning to become unbearable, uncontrollable. "Tsaki, Tsaki, baby," Muzi groaned, over and over again, and Tsakani echoed his rising flood of delight with her own, her voice husky with passion, "Muzi, Muzi, Muzi, my love!"

Completely caught up in the ecstasy of the moment, Muzi found himself marvelling at how free she was, how comfortable and open she was with her body. Even though her stretch marks were clearly visible and her stomach was not entirely flat, there was nothing self-conscious about her. Although Tsakani was nowhere near as beautiful as his wife was, it was evident in the way that she made love that she was confident in her own skin. Poised on top of him, her flaws exposed, a complete absence of any shame in her body made her more desirable.

Impaled on his rock hard shaft, drops of sweat streaming down her face, Tsakani began to grind down and around. They were grinding hard against each other, Muzi's body taut beneath her, his pelvis rising upwards to meet the downward thrusting of her hips onto his throbbing member.

Muzi marvelled at how her flexibility seemed to defy her body shape, and he watched the artsy tattoo in the cave of her right pelvic joint stretching and contracting with her complete surrender to desire. She was moving up and down on him with all the suppleness of a trained belly dancer, and she was driving him wild. The momentum of her gyrating and plunging would increase and alternate, and the walls of her vagina tightened around his penis, making him moan, only to relax and then constrict again, leaving Muzi breathless and amazed at how much control she had over her muscles and walls, massaging and manipulating his cock in a torrid vaginal embrace that left him gasping.

Screaming out each other's names, they climaxed together, the two explosions electrifying the intensity of their simultaneous orgasms. Spent, they collapsed in a heap of entangled limbs. Panting and breathless in the post-orgasmic afterglow, they held onto each other, seductively whispering sweet nothings into each other's ears.

CHAPTER 8

Dusk had settled by the time Muzi arrived home. He and Tsakani had spent most of the day making love, in between talking and eating. He had a chance to take a breather and regain some of his strength when Tsakani got up to make some lunch.

He watched her walk around her apartment naked, in awe of the beauty of being in the presence of a woman who was accepting of her own body, so unlike that which he was accustomed to in his *other life*.

Ever since giving birth to their daughter, Tshidi had become insecure about the slight changes in her supermodel body. Tshidi, truth be told, still had a body that most women would kill or die for, and the flaws she thought she saw in it after childbirth were mostly in her own mind. Muzi could not remember the last time he had seen his wife walking around naked in front of him. Whenever she got out of bed, she would immediately reach for the nearest towel or robe with which to cover herself.

When they made love – or rather *if* they made love, Muzi thought wryly - she had grown wary of any positions which meant that Muzi could see her fully naked. She would joke about it, but she was relentless in her refusal to come on top. "*Hayi* baby, do you want to see these stretch marks of mine and get turned off?" were the kinds of objections Tshidi would come up with, reducing their lovemaking to the missionary position, making Muzi feel as if they were some boring old couple. She kept her bra on during sex, complaining that her breasts were sagging, despite the fact that Muzi thought that they had become fuller and more feminine both with motherhood and with time. They were, in fact, permanently hidden underneath a bra.

If anything, Tsakani was more entitled to complain about droopy breasts. The contrast to Tsakani and the way she exposed her body to Muzi was stark.

Muzi was tired of reassuring his wife that she was still as stunning in the flesh as she had been before childbirth. His assurances only seemed to make Tshidi withdraw deeper into her insecurities and her misgivings about her body. The whole thing had taken its toll on their sex life, but only now that he had started cheating on Tshidi did Muzi realise that the rising sexual frustration was threatening his *commitment* to his marriage.

Between the endless rounds of lovemaking with Tsakani, there had also been quite a bit of talking. Muzi found himself opening up to Tsakani about some of the frustrations in his marriage. Tsakani had amazed him by being prepared to listen, and even to give advice from a woman's point of view. It seemed strange - albeit in an inexplicably beautiful way - that the woman who had just become his *side-chick* was the same woman giving him sage marriage counselling.

The conversation inevitably came around to the thorny topic of whether Muzi would ever consider Tsakani for Tshidi. Tsakani's reaction surprised him.

"Would it make you happy?" she asked, and before he could answer, she continued, "All I know, Muzi, is that I love you and I love making you happy. And I know that if something made you unhappy, I wouldn't want you to do it." She sighed deeply, "Even if that *thing* was you leaving your wife for me. I truly mean that. I love you and all I want is for you to be happy."

Muzi sat there and listened to her speak, wondering silently if he was not lost in his marriage; wondering whether Tsakani was the soul mate that he was supposed to grow old with.

Even though Muzi was suddenly racked by guilt as he arrived home that evening, he soon found himself immersed in the joy of playing with his daughter, who simply assumed that daddy had returned from a day at the office. Tshidi didn't probe him about why he'd had to stay at the office for so long when it was already Christmas break. Perhaps, Muzi thought, observing her out of the corner of his eye, it was because she was too busy WhatsApping or talking on the phone with her friends to even care where he had been all day.

He noticed that supper had not been made. Usually, Muzi would have simply started cooking while Lethu followed him around the kitchen, but today he pretended not to have noticed and continued playing with his daughter in the living room. Besides, he had left Tsakani's place feeling full, and little Lethu had eaten her baby food.

It was around a quarter past eight that evening that Tshidi emerged from her fascination with her phone and asked him, "What should I cook baby? *Yazi*, I just realised that I haven't cooked."

Muzi lied and told her that he'd eaten a late lunch at a place near the office and that he could just as well have a sandwich for supper.

After putting the drowsy Lethu to sleep, Muzi made his own sandwich, ignoring Tshidi when she tried to ask what he would like on his sandwich. Nibbling disinterestedly on the bland sandwich, Tshidi came to sit beside him on the couch in his study. Her phone was not in her hand, and there seemed to be a look of concern on her face. "Is something wrong, my husband?"

Unable to mask the irritation in his voice, Muzi retorted, "Have I done something wrong? Or are you just bored with your friends on the phone now?"

It wasn't *what* he said, but rather the tone of his voice, that alarmed Tshidi. She was not used to hearing him speak to her like that, with none of the usual loving gentleness that was reserved solely for her. Even when they were having arguments, she could always hear the tenderness in his voice.

Tshidi was alarmed. With a woman's unfailing intuition, Tshidi realised that something had happened, and the result of it was that her marriage was in trouble. A small voice – one that would not be silenced - was whispering to her innermost being that her husband was slipping away from her.

Lethu was asleep, and Tshidi felt that she needed to take immediate steps to curb whatever it was that was happening to create this misunderstanding between herself and Muzi.

She coaxed him into bed.

"Muzi, I think maybe I have been neglecting my duties towards you as your wife, as your lover," she said. She loved her husband deeply. Moreover, she knew, in her heart of hearts, that her husband loved her. That she was the love of his life. Whatever had happened, she felt certain that it could be fixed, that they could once again be the happy family they had once been, before motherhood had taken its toll on her self-esteem and her energy levels, and led her to perhaps become neglectful of her husband and his needs.

They made love that night, and Tshidi tried to put her whole self into it, mind, body and soul, but she felt as if Muzi was somehow detached. He seemed to be merely going through the motions, and when he rolled over to go to sleep, she realised that he had not even come inside her.

What Tshidi didn't know, of course, was that her husband had spent the better part of that day reaching intense orgasms with a new lover. Tshidi's mind, however, was unable consider the possibility that another woman was involved.

"He's just been working too hard," she thought. "He'll come around in time. I have to do better by this man. He has been such a devoted husband, lover, friend, and father," she thought, watching him sleep, "I have to do better."

Tshidi woke up that Saturday morning with fresh resolve. Muzi was surprised to find himself being treated to a huge breakfast in bed. He was even more surprised, as the lazy morning stretched out, to notice that her phone was not constantly in her hand. When he commented about this, asking if she was having problems with her WhatsApp, Tshidi said the words that he had longed for a long time to hear her say. "This phone and my friends have been stealing my time with my family. I want you to know, my love, that I'm going to be making some changes. I know that I have been taking you for granted, that I have been taking advantage of what a wonderful and dedicated husband and father you have been in this house to our little family. I promise to be better. I promise *to do* better."

Muzi looked into her eyes and remembered why he had fallen in love with her all those years ago.

While they were talking, Lethu woke up and started crying for attention. Instinctively, Muzi rose to attend to her, but Tshidi got up instead, telling him to relax. "I want you to rest my love," she said, "I'm not joking when I say a lot of things are gonna change around here. I love you, and losing you would kill me, *baba ka Lethu.*"

She gave him a lingering kiss before leaving the room. He watched her go out, and it struck him again what a beautiful woman she was.

His conscience, once again, was getting the better of him. No, Muzi decided, there was no way that he could ever leave his beautiful wife who had given him such a beautiful daughter. There was just no way. As wonderful as Tsakani was, he simply could not break up this family - his family - for her. Or could he?

CHAPTER 9

Finding himself in a situation that he had never imagined being in - cheating on his wife - Muzi desperately tried to make sense of what was happening to him. How had it become possible for him to do the very thing he'd sworn he would never do as a married man? The very thing that he despised in other married men. How many friends had he cut off simply because they were married just like him but behaved as if cheating on their wives was the normal, acceptable thing to do?

He had lost count.

Was it that he had genuine, undeniable feelings for Tsakani, or was it just his sexual frustrations playing themselves out?

Without excusing himself entirely, he was aware that his infidelity was the result of the sexual spark that had gone missing in his marriage. There had been a time when he had refused to allow this to bother him. He would convince himself that Tshidi's sudden lack of interest in lovemaking had something to do with her being recently introduced to the motherhood club.

He had even googled the term *post-natal depression* in an attempt to understand the changes in his wife since she'd given birth to Lethu. There had been some information about a loss of interest in sex, which was related to the physical changes a woman experiences after giving birth. Tshidi had become self-conscious about her body; Muzi had seen it in the way she kept herself covered up around the house. On the few occasions that she was naked in his presence, it was because she thought that he was asleep. Muzi would pretend to be asleep so that he could watch his wife undress. If she noticed that he was awake, she would quickly cover up. What did it all mean?

Muzi missed the days when they used to sit around or lie in bed, completely naked, making love and gossiping in between, as all couples do. But most of all, he missed the sex. He missed the *meaningful* sex terribly. It hurt and frustrated him that Tshidi had begun to see it as some kind of chore; like she was doing it *just nje*[12], because Muzi was her husband and he had his needs, but it meant little more to her than that to her. Gone was the Tshidi who used to send him an SMS during the day to tell him what she wanted to do to him later that night. He had forgotten what it felt like to be wanted by his wife; to be appreciated and enjoyed by the love of his life.

Muzi had, at one point, asked Tshidi if she didn't think that she was suffering from post-natal depression. He had suggested to her that there was no shame in seeing a professional, a psychologist perhaps, if she felt that she was struggling.

But his concern had been laughed off on more than one occasion. She either said that she was fine, or she

---

[12] Translated literally as *just because, with little or no enthusiasm*

said that she would be fine *soon* and that he shouldn't be concerned. He worried too much, she often said. "You over-think things, my love," brushing him off, "It's that brilliant brain of yours, it works overtime sometimes."

Muzi was well aware that sex wasn't the only thing that Tshidi seemed to have lost interest in (or simply stopped trying to do with any kind of enthusiasm or commitment). He thought about how she had begun to take on less and less responsibility around the house. The Tshidi, who used to take pride in cooking him his favourite meals, had disappeared. Her domestic responsibilities were conducted mechanically, with little or no energy, and it seemed to be getting worse as time moved on.

Muzi had never been one of these men who refused to help around the house. He had no problem with cooking and cleaning, and it hardly bothered him at first when he noticed that Tshidi was no longer doing her fair share of the chores. Muzi was a doting father, and Lethu was a daddy's girl, so it could never be argued that Tshidi was always tired from having to look after their baby. And besides, they had employed a nanny.

Hope was the only thing that got him through from one day to another. He would reassure himself that it was nothing more than a passing phase in their marriage and that they would soon return to their previous routine of wild, passionate sex, instead of it being only him that was interested; it was always Muzi who did the initiating.

Added to this, and to his great disappointment, Tshidi had taken to coming to bed in a onesie. It was as if she was sending him a not-so-subtle message: *Don't touch.*

There was one thing that was Muzi knew for certain: He was sexually frustrated. He was being starved of the one thing that a man could not do without. No matter what he did, their sex life continued to deteriorate.

"Perhaps that is why I have fallen for Tsakani," he pondered, trying to find an answer that would validate his behaviour.

CHAPTER 10

It would be difficult to see Tsakani over the Christmas holidays. Work could no longer be used as a valid and readily available excuse whenever he wanted to slip out of the house. Besides, Muzi wasn't even sure that he wanted this thing with Tsakani to continue. The fact that he was becoming - or had, in fact, become - the very type of man that for so long he had despised, irked him. The whole situation had become his worst nightmare.

But, he couldn't deny it; the time that he was spending with Tsakani was proving to be a beautiful nightmare, if there was such a thing. With Tsakani, he felt desired, loved, and important. She made him feel like Tshidi had once made him feel: like the centre of her world.

With Tshidi now visibly aware of the fact that she had been slacking, and her promises to make more of an effort to appreciate him ever prevalent, he continued questioning whether it was not an opportune time – especially considering he would be removed from his work environment for a full two weeks – to break it off with Tsakani.

But yet he longed for Tsakani. He craved her touch, her warmth, and her unashamed need for him. Despite his better judgment, he would catch himself devising ways and means of getting away from home to spend time with her. Thoughts of the wild, beautiful love they had made filled him with longing and left his manhood hard, throbbing with desire.

The logical part of him desperately wanted him to put an end to this delicious affair and dedicate himself to fixing his marriage, whereas another part of him refused to listen to common sense, and plagued him with tales that told of a miserable life without Tsakani, where neither one could live without the other.

The two had been communicating daily via WhatsApp, and even though Tsakani had made it clear to Muzi how much she missed him, she understood that he couldn't just leave home to spend time with her, especially during the Christmas break, which was, traditionally, a time for family.

Tshidi and Muzi were sitting at the burnished oak table in the dining room eating breakfast one morning, when Muzi received a phone call from his childhood friend, Zolani. Zolani and Muzi had grown up together in Witbank, and their friendship had stood the test of time, despite the long distance that they lived from each other.

Zolani was one of those guys who hadn't been very lucky in life. He had not managed to escape the cycle of poverty into which he had been born, and, after high school - when most of his friends, including Muzi, had managed to get into tertiary institutions through bursaries and family support - Zolani remained behind, forced to take up whatever jobs he could find. His parents had been poor, elderly and sick, and, being the eldest, Zolani was responsible for taking care of his siblings. There were mouths to feed, and any dreams that he might have had of going off to college - even with his average grades - vanished into thin air.

Muzi and Musa, who had been his best friends growing up, had remained close to him and helped him out wherever they could, even after university when employment had sent them into exile in Johannesburg, the City of Gold, leaving Zolani in the Place of Coal – Emalahleni - as Witbank had since been renamed. *The Three Musketeers,* the name by which they had referred to themselves as since their Primary School days, were more like family than friends.

Zolani had called to tell Muzi about the death of one of his younger brothers. He had been stabbed in a tavern the night before.

There was plenty to be discussed with respect to the funeral arrangements, especially with money being an issue. For starters, the mortuary and undertakers would have to be paid. Zolani and Muzi discussed these and other related issues while Muzi's breakfast grew cold on his plate.

After hanging up, and although he was quite sure that Tshidi had heard the gist of what the phone call was about, he explained the situation in great detail. She knew Zolani from the few times that she'd been to Witbank with Muzi, and she knew how close they were.

Without really thinking it through, Muzi assumed that Tshidi would attend the funeral with him. Whether they would take Lethu with them or leave her with Tshidi's parents in Daveyton would be a separate discussion.

The funeral was arranged for the following Saturday, with a night vigil to be the night before. Catching Muzi off guard the Thursday night before they were due to leave for the funeral, Tshidi suddenly announced that she wasn't planning to accompany him.

Muzi did a double take. True, she had never been a fan of visiting Witbank, but, well, this wasn't exactly a visit, was it? It was something that had to be done, in the name of decency, friendship, loyalty, and, above all, responsibility. Had she not, just recently, been talking about being more supportive?

His disappointment was short-lived as it gave way to a grand opportunity, one where he could – without raising any suspicions - take a drive and spend a night with Tsakani.

Muzi also realised that Tsakani could accompany him to Witbank. Not to the funeral, but he could book her into a hotel with him, spend the night with her after a couple of hours at the night vigil, and drive back with her after the funeral on Saturday. When he called to suggest this plan to Tsakani, she was over the moon with joy and excitement. Muzi dispelled his rising feelings of guilt on the day of their departure by reasoning that it was Tshidi's sudden reluctance to accompany him that had made this getaway possible to begin with.

When he arrived at Tsakani's place to fetch her, he was pleasantly surprised to see that she had bought sacks of potatoes and cabbage, as well as a sizeable amount of frozen meat. He'd told her about the material circumstances of Zolani and his family and may have mentioned that he would have to help out with supplies and payments. It was customary amongst his people to do this kind of thing. Tsakani's kindness and consideration surprised him and left him glowing anew over what an incredibly thoughtful and caring woman she was. What she had done was not necessary, but it was most certainly appreciated. In the back of his mind, it bothered Muzi that Tshidi had not thought to perform a similar gesture before he left. Doing something thoughtful for somebody who was important to *him* was, quite simply, unimportant to her.

Driving to Witbank, she stroked his thigh and told him about the things she couldn't wait to do to him later that night - after the night vigil - when she had him all to herself.

Driving to Zolani's parent's township home that evening, Muzi was quite certain that Tsakani was the sexiest woman he'd ever met. It was something more than her looks; it was a feminine yet free demeanour about her sexuality and how much she enjoyed making love to him; it was something in the tenderness of her touch when she stroked him, and the husky honesty in her voice when she spoke to him that made her irresistible.

Zolani greeted Muzi as he entered the family home. The coffin had arrived earlier that evening and was laid out in the main bedroom. Members of the community had gathered to help the family with the funeral preparations. Three-legged cast iron pots had been placed on the fires outside. The women chopped and peeled vegetables on long trestle tables while the men prepared a cow for slaughter.

Muzi knew that he could not stay for more than a few hours, but he made himself useful enough that he could quietly slip away and get back to Tsakani before it got too late.

That night, she gave him an evening to remember. She was waiting up for him in a racy black number when he returned to the hotel. She slowly began to undress him, placing a provocative finger against his lips when he tried to speak. "Shush, my love, there'll be time enough to talk later," she said, kissing him down his chest as she slowly unbuttoned his shirt and then his pants, "We've got *all* night."

Leading him to the bed, she purred evocatively, "I know just what you need, I've got you." She gently laid him face down on the bed and began massaging his shoulders, working her way down his back. Her touch was light and then firm, kneading as she stroked and teased him, working the tension out of knots that Muzi hadn't even known that he had. By the time she began to massage his firm buttocks, he was literally on fire, while being completely relaxed.

"Oh, baby, Tsakani, your touch is magic,' he moaned as she turned him around and jacked his throbbing manhood slowly with one hand, while the other played with his nipples. Her cherry red nails were grazing his erect nipples, making him grimace with the sheer pleasure of it all. He wanted to take her then and there, mount her, but Tsakani, teasing him, moved away and got off the bed.

She stood there looking flushed and radiant, her lips parted with arousal, and hiked the tiny black negligee she had on above her hips, gyrating her lower body and giving him an impromptu lap dance while he throbbed with desire.

"Come here, Muzi, lover boy," she whispered, and pulled him up from the bed, "Come here, you beautiful man."

She led him out onto the balcony, which Muzi hadn't seen when they had booked in that morning. It was a warm summer night, with a sultry breeze caressing their skin. Tsakani gently pushed him down onto a sleeper chair on the balcony, and Muzi could see the lights coming from other rooms of the guesthouse. The possibility that they could be seen – and in all likelihood *would* be seen, if anyone wandered out onto the balcony of their own room, or even so much as drew a curtain to look outside - only added to the heat and passion of the moment.

She lifted her black negligee up above her hips, and this time went all the way up, over her head, and tossed it to one side as her full breasts glimmered in the moonlight. She pulling him upright so that he was in a sitting position, and proceeded to straddle him, lowering herself onto his rigid member. Muzi felt the soft, tight velvet sheathing of her labia grasping his shaft in a chokehold grip. He smothered her breasts, one and then the other, in his mouth as she bore down on him, moaning with pleasure and a tinge of pain as he entered her completely.

"Oh, Tsakani, Tsakani, my love," Muzi groaned, out of his mind in the ecstasy of the moment. She began to ride him expertly, deep, and then pausing to all the tip of his penis to playing tantalisingly at the entrance to her pulsating lips, up, down, up, down, arching her back as they climaxed in unison, calling out each other's names.

Back inside the hotel room, they continued to make love. Each time Muzi thought he was truly and completely spent, Tsakani somehow knew just where and how to touch him, which buttons to press. Within seconds he would feel himself growing hard again and they would find themselves entangled in each other, their limbs melting into each other, over and over again until they were both glistening with sweat and hoarse with thirst from their husky screams and moans.

Tsakani got up to pour a glass of ice-cold cranberry juice from the bar fridge in the room. Muzi was again struck by how comfortable she was in and with her body and all its imperfections, making her infinitely more beautiful and sexy than she might have been otherwise.

Muzi had an early start the following morning and set his alarm for 6am. Before they dozed off, the small talk came around to how they would continue seeing each other during the holidays. They would figure something out, they both agreed.

The subject of his being married came up, and, to lighten up the mood, Muzi told her a joke that Zolani had once told him: A man had once arrived home from work unannounced. Going upstairs, he hears his wife's moans from their bedroom and shouts in concern while running up the remaining stairs. He finds his wife on the bed, naked, sweating, and convulsing as she was having an epileptic fit. Seeing him in the doorway, she stammers that she thinks she's having a heart attack. The man hurriedly wraps his wife in a sheet and carries her downstairs, calling for the helper to phone for an ambulance. While the helper is giving frantic directions over the phone, he rushes upstairs again to get a gown for his wife, only to find his brother, who was renovating their mansion, standing naked out on the bedroom's balcony. He starts shouting while grabbing his wife's gown, "Steve, you damn fool, my wife might be having a heart attack and here you are running around naked instead of calling an ambulance. You bloody idiot!"

Tsakani laughed at his joke. She laughed until the tears were streaming down her face. "You're so funny," she said, trying – and failing - to stop her laughter.

Muzi suddenly remembered, with surprising clarity, how he'd once told the same joke to Tshidi not long after he'd heard it from Zolani. He remembered her languid attempt at laughing; thinking then that perhaps the joke wasn't as funny as he'd thought it was, or that perhaps he simply could not tell it in as funny a way as Zolani had.

His somewhat sad remembrance of that moment vanished as quickly as it had appeared.

He held Tsakani tightly in his arms; the woman who thought that he was the funniest man in the world.

CHAPTER 11

The sun was breaking over the horizon when Muzi woke to the sound of his alarm going off. The sheets were creased from where Tsakani had been sleeping next to him, but she was not there. She was standing alongside the bed, ironing his shirt for the funeral. She had set her alarm slightly earlier and had placed her phone under her pillow, not wanting to wake him when it went off. "I want you to look good today, baby," she said, smiling from behind a cloud of steam, "And your shirt was creased. I couldn't allow you to leave like that."

Muzi could not remember when he had last felt taken care of like this. Tshidi was the kind of wife who planned her outfit the night before but couldn't find Lethu's shoes in the morning. Tsakani struck him as the kind of woman who would plan her outfit the night before, but she would keep everybody else in mind too.

Tsakani slipped back into bed beside him and snuggled into his chest. She knew that it wouldn't be long before he had to leave for the funeral, and they had to check out by 10am.

Muzi found himself confiding in Tsakani about Tshidi's reluctance to spend their holidays at his paternal home in Witbank.

Muzi witnessed Tsakani becoming openly – and vocally - critical of his wife. She was appalled by Tshidi's behaviour.

"*Hawu*, what married woman doesn't look forward to spending time with her in-laws?" she asked, visibly annoyed, "She's mad. I really cannot understand her. I *look forward* to the time I spend with mine, and I take great pride in helping out when I am there. This is not the first time I've said this."

Perhaps it all boiled down to the fact that Tshidi was a taker, and Tsakani was a giver, Muzi thought. But no, Tshidi had not been like this before they were married; she had always been a generous and helpful person around his family during their courtship. Ironically, it appeared that motherhood had drained her of her sense of family responsibility.

Even on those rare occasions after Lethu's birth when Tshidi would recover her spark, it was her friends who benefitted, rather than her immediate family. That *blasted* phone in her hand, he thought angrily; if she wasn't speaking on it, she was WhatsApping on it. That phone had become a barrier between them.

Muzi shared how relieved Tshidi had been to return to work - she no longer had to explain an unkempt house and uncooked meals – and how slowly, almost imperceptibly, he had become the principal caregiver of his daughter.

What he failed to share with Tsakani was how Tshidi had recently promised to change how she approached her responsibilities as a wife and mother, and that he was fighting an inner batter over ending his affair with Tsakani and dedicating himself to rebuilding his family.

But it was time to leave. Muzi winked and blew Tsakani a kiss from the bedroom door. "I won't be long," he said huskily.

"There's no rush, baby," she teased, "This girl needs some rest. You *punished* me last night!"

Having arrived in Witbank with his side-chick instead of his wife, and with a ten o'clock check out from the hotel looming, Muzi knew that staying after the funeral to catch up with his old friends was not going to happen.

Throughout the funeral, Muzi found his thoughts wandering back to Tsakani, his body prickling with sexual electricity as he relived the previous night's exploits in his mind. And then his thoughts would drift back to Tshidi and Lethu; the reality that, in a few hours, he would have to face.

The drive ahead of them was a good two hours, and although they were each lost in their own thoughts, it was a comfortable silence. Tsakani was reading the latest issue of Drum magazine and had her feet up on the dashboard. She hummed to Nina Simone from behind her dark designer sunglasses. Muzi glanced over at her and thought about the times when it was Tshidi sitting beside him on those long road trips.

The sun was setting on the dusty Jozi horizon that welcomed them home later that afternoon, the sky a fresco of pinks and oranges and purples. Parked outside Tsakani's apartment, Muzi carried her luggage up the staircase. They stood in the doorway and embraced.

"I know," sighed Tsakani, reading the look in his eyes, "It's back to reality."

Muzi breathed in deeply and squeezed her hand. "You're incredible," he said.

"I had a really good time," she said and smiled.

Muzi let go of Tsakani's hand and turned and walked slowly back down the stairs towards his car. He looked up and saw her standing at the window. He pressed the ignition and pushed his foot down on the accelerator. It was time to go home.

He glanced at himself in the rearview mirror. *I'm living like a rat*, he thought to himself, remembering the words of his late uncle. "As a grown man," his uncle would say, "Never find yourself having to live like a rat." But here he was, Muzi, the once faithful husband, living in the shadows. Instead of being able to walk in through the front door of his home with a clear conscience, he was now going to walking in carrying a dark secret. He would have to watch his every move. His phone would always have to be placed facing down.

Muzi was suddenly overwhelmed with a fear of Tshidi finding out about his infidelity. He drove his car into the underground parking garage of a nearby shopping centre and found an empty section where nobody was parked. He switched off the ignition. Rummaging through his car and under the seats, he inspected it for evidence. He got out and opened the boot. Unzipping his suitcase, he unpacked and repacked his clothes and toiletries. *The condoms*, he thought, *had he remembered to get rid of them?* He slipped his hands down the inner compartments of his luggage and felt around, checking and rechecking. *No*, he recalled, *he had thrown them away*. He zipped the suitcase up again and slammed the boot shut. Sitting in the driver's seat, he wondered if Tshidi would be able to smell Tsakani's perfume on him. He wondered how much lying he would be doing in the days and the weeks that lay ahead. He wondered how many tracks he would need to cover. Would one night away from his wife lead to others? He was living the best of both worlds, but he risked being caught. And that risk meant that he would be living like a rat.

Opening the front door to his home and stepping inside, Muzi felt ill. His stomach was turning. But Tshidi welcomed him with open arms. She had, it seemed, genuinely missed him.

That evening, Muzi found himself overcome with an insatiable desire for his wife. Tshidi and Muzi made love with a passion and enthusiasm that Muzi last remembered experiencing in their earlier days as lovers before marital responsibilities and parenthood had begun to consume their lives. It felt as if they were rediscovering each other's bodies; what they enjoyed and how they felt about each other. Muzi wondered whether Tsakani had had any influence over his newfound, unquenchable sexual appetite.

Tsakani lurked at the back of Muzi's mind. He thought briefly about opening up to Tshidi about his brief fling, but then quickly decided against it. What harm could his infidelity have on his wife is she knew nothing of it? Besides, he didn't want to burden the beauty of the new lease of life their marriage was experiencing with the spectre of his foolish indiscretion.

Once again, Muzi's thoughts returned to ending the affair. Stepping down from his role as the betrayer seemed easier when he was not in Tsakani's alluring presence. He had to find a way of telling her that he would not be cheating on his wife again.

Waking to the sound of his phone vibrating the following morning, Muzi rolled over in bed and, wiping the sleep out of his eyes, read Tsakani's message.

Hey boo,

Had so much fun.

Can't stop thinking about you.

Hope to see you soon.

Muzi considered replying immediately, breaking it to her that their affair would have to end, but no, he thought, a text message would be too impersonal and cruel. Tsakani had done nothing more than love him, even though she knew that he was spoken for. She deserved to hear it in person.

"Who was that?" Tshidi asked, flicking through the television channels. Muzi felt himself breaking out into a cold sweat. Turning the phone onto its face on his bedside table, he caught his breath. "It was Zolani," he said, "He was just checking in to make sure I got home safely."

"Oh, okay," she replied, none the wiser.

Rat, he thought. All he wanted to do was get out of the house, and fast.

"Do we have eggs in the house, baby?" he asked, sitting up. Lethu walked up to his bedside table and picked up Muzi's phone. She loved watching cartoons on it. The message was still open. He hadn't had time to delete it.

"We bought groceries yesterday, baby," Tshidi answered, rolling over towards Muzi, resting her head in his lap.

Muzi lifted Lethu up onto the bed and took his phone out of her hands. "I'm just going to take my phone to the study," he said to Tshidi, "I don't want her playing on it while I'm in the shower."

Walking down the passageway, Muzi quickly replied to Tsakani's message, telling her he would be over later that morning. Careful to cover his tracks, he deleted all traces of their conversation from his phone and headed back to the bedroom to take a shower.

"I'm going out to have a few drinks with the boys," he announced to Tshidi before he closed the bathroom door. The festive season often involved what his friends referred to as *iiBig Days*, where there was no set time for what time or day one would start drinking.

"Okay, baby," Tshidi replied. Lethu was agitated. Tshidi decided to go and fetch some paper and crayons from the study so that Lethu could keep herself busy until her daddy emerged from the shower.

Tshidi noticed the message that had just come through on her husband's phone.

You had better make sure that you have enough energy to keep up with me today because I'm planning on exhausting you in bed, boo, it read.

Tshidi quickly replaced the phone on the study desk and, shaking, grabbed the box of crayons and a few sheets of paper and returned to the bedroom. She picked Lethu up and took her through to the TV room.

Hearing her husband's footsteps walking down the passageway to the front door, Tshidi called out to him, "Love, you forgot your phone in the study."

With so many business projects in the offing, his desk was cluttered with paper. Muzi was hardly surprised that he had completely missed his phone on his way out.

He wondered why Tshidi was suddenly so interested in his phone. Perhaps this was her way of being more attentive and considerate, he thought.

But, what if, while he was showering…?

No, he reasoned, promptly banishing the thought from his mind, Tshidi trusted him way too much to go snooping around on his phone.

Retrieving his phone from the study, he walked down to the TV room, where Lethu was on the floor, playing with her toys. Tshidi was bent down on the floor with her, pretending to be some sort of animal, and Lethu was pretending to slay her with a plastic sword. Daddy's girl was already showing a liking for boys' games, Muzi thought as he stood in the doorway watching the two of them play.

He suddenly felt overcome with a powerful feeling of pride and joy as a husband and a father, realising that they were going to be okay as a family after all. Tshidi had been serious about changing. His beautiful, attentive wife was herself again; happy, crawling around with their daughter on the tiles and imitating the sound of whatever animal she was supposed to be in their world of make-believe. This was the same Tshidi who had, not so long ago, been completely preoccupied with her phone. Her constant Whatsapping and not wanting to be bothered was indeed a thing of the past.

All that was required of Muzi was to go and end this little spell of madness with Tsakani and return home.

Home, yes, he thought, smiling contentedly, *back home where the heart is…*

"You going already, baby?" Tshidi asked, scooping Lethu up off the floor. Muzi kissed his daughter goodbye, "Daddy's coming back soon, my princess, *uyezwa?*" [13]He took Lethu from Tshidi and enveloped her in one of his tight bear hugs that always made her squeal with delight. *Daddy* was going to be coming home for good. He was coming home to be a husband and a father.

Tshidi walked him to the front door. He reminded her that he was just catching a few drinks with the boys and that he would be back in a couple of hours. They kissed, and, as he turned to leave, he felt her hand lightly on his arm.

"Are you okay, my love?" he asked, searching her face for an answer. He could not quite make out what he was seeing in her eyes. Tshidi was silent for a moment.

"Baby, we're okay, aren't we?" she asked, almost hesitantly, "I mean, you and me?"

Muzi kissed her forehead and hugged her in a tight embrace. "Baby, we're *better* than just *okay*, do you hear me?" He pulled her closer and gently lifted her

---

[13] A promise

chin, looking her directly in the eyes, "I promise you, my love, Tshidi, my wife, we're better than just okay. Okay? I love you. I'll be back before you can even miss me."

He kissed his wife full on the lips and walked towards his car. He had to end this thing with Tsakani, he thought resolutely, and he had to end it today.

CHAPTER 12

Arriving at Tsakani's apartment, Muzi was greeted with a vision of temptation. Red lace knickers, a red bra, and red lipstick on a set of voluptuous lips. Tsakani quickly pulled him inside.

"Do you have any idea how much I've missed you, mister?" she whispered, fumbling with his belt. Muzi made a half-hearted attempt to push her away. He was standing on a Persian rug in the little hallway of her exquisitely furnished loft. "Tsakani, we really need to talk," he mumbled, feeling his belt fly free while her expert hand dived into his crotch. He could feel himself throbbing with hardness. She kneeled before him. Muzi noticed the drawn blinds, the rose petals scattered around the leather settee upon which they had first made love. The shadows of the candles flickered and danced across the walls.

"We can always talk later, my love," she whispered, her voice hoarse from wanting him.

A pang of pain and a prick of lust mingled into a state of confused helplessness, making him weak with desire. His hands were cupped around her face. He wanted to pull her up and push her away, but he felt powerless to resist. Tsakani had taken him into her mouth, her velvet lips enveloping the hardness of his cock while he clutched at her hair, which cascaded over her shoulders in long braids; pulling her head closer in.

She teased the tip of his penis with her tongue, covered his head with her lips; her nails scraping languorously over his scrotum while she kissed and sucked him, sweeping him up in a frenzy of ecstasy. Muzi closed his eyes, clenching his teeth. Something was rising from deep within him, aching for release, pumping and pulsing through every nerve ending of the tight knot that was his body, and Tsakani could feel his momentum building. She pulled back just a little and allowed her teeth to graze over the tip of his blazing manhood.

"Yes baby, yes, come for me, come inside my mouth big boy," she whispered huskily. Muzi began to moan uncontrollably. She pout-kissed the tip of his penis, clamping her lips along the length of him, taking him deep into her mouth. Muzi felt himself explode, like the swollen banks of a dam bursting inside her mouth.

Tsakani licked him clean, and Muzi felt his breathing slowly returning to normal. How would he proceed now, he wondered, the fog in his head starting to lift? *Could* he proceed now? *Should* he, right now? How? What could he say, or do, right now, to complete his mission of breaking up with her?

"You're very quiet, my darling," Tsakani said, looking up at him, her eyes filled with love. Muzi felt his heart leap into a painful spasm as it clawed its way up his throat. He swallowed hard. He felt his lips part, and then the words, "Tsakani, we really need to talk."

She buried her braids in the pit of muscle between his shoulder and his neck. He felt her body tremble and shudder, and then he felt her stiffen with tension, followed by the rush of warm fluid as her tears flooded their way down his neck and on to his chest. Her pain was palpable. Almost unbearable. "Don't cry Tsakani. Please don't cry," he whispered.

She sat up and pushed him away, disentangling herself from their now-awkward embrace and walked over to the leather settee, throwing herself onto it and dissolving into loud, open-mouthed sobs. Between her tears and her heartrending cries, she blurted out the words that she did not want to ever hear herself say, "You're leaving me, aren't you? You are! Say it! Say it Muzi! I know you are, so just say it!"

An uneasy silence settled over the apartment, punctuated by Tsakani's sobbing and Muzi's deeply conflicted sighs.

"Tsakani, my wife and my daughter, they're my family," he said apprehensively, unable to look Tsakani directly in the eyes, "They're my whole world." He gathered his clothes from the floor and pulled his pants back on. He could feel her eyes boring into to him. "I'm so sorry that I got you entangled in this mess, Tsakani, but I could never leave my wife. Not ever."

Suddenly there was a knock at the door. "Are you expecting anyone?" Muzi asked, almost in a whisper, joining her on the leather sofa.

"It's probably just one of the maintenance staff," she said, rising from the sofa and disappearing into her bedroom. She emerged covered in a full-length nightgown and walked to the door. Peering through the peephole, Muzi waited in silence.

"Muzi, how does your wife know that you're here?" Tsakani had turned around and was walking towards him. "That's her at the door. I recognise her from the photos on your desk at work. What does she want here? What is she doing at my place?"

Muzi leapt off the sofa in a blind panic and ran into Tsakani's bedroom, slamming the door behind him and pressing himself up against it. His heart was thumping loudly in his throat and it felt as if one hundred stallions were galloping across his torso. He held his breath and listened intently for any sounds coming from beyond the door. He heard as Tsakani opened the front door, much to his despair and confusion. *Why would she do that*, he thought.

"Muzi!" Tshidi shouted, her footsteps moving through the apartment, "Muzi! Muzi! I know you're in here, Muzi!" Suddenly fists were banging on the bedroom door against which his back was pressed. He was trembling. She was right there. "Muzi!" her voice echoed, "Open this door! Open it now!" And then, "Is he in there, you bitch? Bitch! I'm talking to you, bitch! Is my husband behind this door?"

There was silence. Tsakani had not uttered a single word since Tshidi's explosive entry. Backing away from the door, Muzi swung himself around and opened it. "I'm here, Tshidi," he said, stepping quickly out of the bedroom and into the living area.

Tsakani was sitting on the leather sofa, her head in her hands. Muzi faced his furious wife, setting his jaw with the sincerity of the effort. "We've been having an affair for a few weeks. I came here today to end it," he said firmly, swallowing hard, "I'm sorry Tshidi, I'm sorry my love."

Tsakani remained motionless, although Muzi, with mounting dread, almost expected her to contradict him by mentioning what had just happened between them.

Tshidi pulled up a seat from the chair-desk-mirror combo just outside the bedroom door and sat down. An uneasy silence enveloped the trio. For what seemed like an eternity, not a word was spoken. Muzi's ears were ringing, and his heart was thumping in his throat. Eventually, Tshidi cleared her throat and spoke, turning towards and addressing Tsakani directly.

"Listen to me *sisi*[14]," she said, "I think I recognise you from Muzi's workplace. Muzi is my husband, and I know that he has done both of us wrong, but please,

---

[14] Sister

let me leave with my husband. And please," she said, a sharp edge of caution in her voice, "Please forget about him. For the sake of our family. For the sake of peace."

Tsakani did not respond. She was eerily quiet and Muzi wondered whether a fight was going to break out between the two women.

Tshidi stood up and motioned to Muzi. "Muzi, my husband, let's go home. We should go home *now*." Muzi could not bring himself to look at either of the women. He nodded, his eyes facing the floor, and walked towards the door. All he wanted to do was to go home, as Tshidi had suggested. Nothing mattered anymore. It was time to face the music.

Although Tshidi appeared calm, he knew that it was probably the quiet before the storm. He knew he could not risk losing his wife and his family over what had happened. Muzi didn't care about how long Tshidi might make him pay for his infidelity, or how she would exact her revenge. He would atone for his sins. He would do whatever was necessary to save his marriage.

Tshidi walked to the open door, pausing in the doorway, motioning towards Muzi to say goodbye to his 'friend'.

"I want to hear you say it," she said.

"Goodbye, Tsakani," Muzi said. Tsakani raised her head, her face streaked with tears. "Goodbye, Muzi," she answered softly.

Muzi and Tshidi left Tsakani's apartment and walked towards his car. "I took an Uber," Tshidi said, anticipating his question. They stood together alongside his car, neither getting in.

"I left Lethu at my mom's place," she added.

Muzi nodded. Suddenly Tshidi's phone started ringing. Tshidi glanced down at the number and answered the call.

"Yes, yes," she said, "I managed to find it, thank you, it was exactly where I'd left it," and then she laughed and added, "I am never drinking wine again. Thank you for all your help!"

She ended the call and Muzi looked at her questioningly.

"Tracker," she said, "That's how I knew where you were."

Suddenly overcome with emotion, Tshidi began to sob. Muzi took her into his arms and embraced her, right there on the street. "Tshidi, I love you, baby," he whispered, wiping the tears from her face, "I'm so sorry."

"I know you love me, my husband," Tshidi replied, pulling away from him and opening the passenger door, "Let's go home."

Tshidi's right hand tenderly caressed the back of her husband's neck, his eyes focused on the road. She felt her phone vibrate and she looked down at the screen.

"I miss you, sexy," it read, followed by three red hearts.

Tshidi turned her phone to face downwards. Muzi took his eyes off the road and looked at Tshidi, acknowledging his wife lovingly. He could not believe how much this woman loved him; he was astounded at her capacity to forgive.

#AlongCameThemba

ACKNOWLEDGEMENTS

I would like to thank the men who were willing to share their personal stories with me.

A special thank you to everyone who held my hand during this process of becoming a first-time author. To my manager Vanessa Tloubatla, Deborah Du Plooy, Phillipa Mitchell, Perfect Hlongwane, Naksconcepts, my family, my wife Liza and my daughters Tshimollo and Motheo, thank you for your endless support and for allowing me the space and time to be creative.

Thank you to everyone who will buy or has purchased this book. I hope it helps you in some way.

I can't wait to share the sequel with you, and I hope that it will have the same impact on men as this book has on women.

ABOUT THE AUTHOR

Kagiso Modupe, a BSc Sport Science graduate, is a well-known South African born actor, radio host and motivational speaker.

He is also a successful television and film director and producer, musician, entrepreneur, and Brothers for Life ambassador.

A passionate humanitarian, Kagiso works with various non-profit organisations across South Africa to uplift the lives of the youth through the arts, through sport and through entrepreneurship.

Along came Tsakani is his first published work.